SUNDAYS WITH MUNDY

with Love
Jim

GRATITUDE FOR JON AND "SUNDAY WITH MUNDY"

I thoroughly enjoy your Sunday writings! I love this passage from today's epistle, "…even the wrong road is the right road when it leads us to a turning point." **Dr. Lee Jampolsky,** author of *Smile for No Good Reason*

Read this book with your heart open, and your mind stilled of all outside thoughts. It will bring you into a Circle of Light as a deep inner wisdom and understanding of *A Course in Miracles* is revealed.
Beth Geer, author of *Awakening To One Love* and *Awakening Humanity: Our Place Among Extraterrestrials and Angels.*

I so appreciate the clarity of your writing. You are such a gift, and I feel blessed to know you. Thank you for all you do.
Patricia Pearce, author of *Beyond Jesus: My Spiritual Journey*

I love the writings you send. Especially, when I am not feeling my best. Thank you so much, Jon. It all makes sense. **Rev. Angela J. Wright**

Thank you for this beautiful lesson. Your messages are nuggets of wisdom and resonate deeply with me. I always endeavor to live by the spiritual truths of the Course, which you so generously share with us.
Rev. Steve Jarose

Thank you, Jon. How fortunate we are to wake up on Sunday mornings with your inspiring words. It is always a wonderful surprise for me.
Loretta McGrath

Jon, This, is a beautiful writing/reading you have created today. Makes my Sunday! **Lydia Swan,** Lexington MA

Thank you so much dear Jon, today it was exactly what I needed to read. God bless you for your help and services. **Fani Mylona,** Greece

Your words today were taken into my heart and will be my sustaining thoughts today. You express truth in a way that makes things clear and meaningful to me. Thank you. **Sheila,** Vero Beach, FL

Dear Jon, Thank you so much for your Sunday thoughts. Somehow you always pick just what I needed to read. **Astrid Larson**

Thank you from the bottom of my heart, for the kind and clear meaning in your Sunday words. I read the Sunday letter with joy and calmness enters in my heart! **Gabrielle Kamber,** Grateful

I love every missive you send out, and this week is no exception.
Rev. Dr. Bud James, Reno, NV

SUNDAYS WITH MUNDY

Inspiration for the Inner Journey

JON MUNDY, Ph. D.

COGENT PUBLISHING NY

Published by Cogent Publishing NY
Imprint of The Whitson Group, Inc.
3770 Barger Street, Unit 604
Shrub Oak, NY 10588
USA
(845) 528-7617

Copyright © 2023 Jon Mundy

ALL RIGHTS RESERVED. No part of this book may be reproduced or transmitted in any form or by any means, electronic or mechanical, including photocopying, recording, video, or by any information and retrieval system, without the prior written permission from the publisher. The scanning, uploading and distribution of this book via the Internet or via any other means without the prior written permission of the publisher is illegal and punishable by law.

A Course in Miracles material used in this book comes from the ACIM Third Edition published by the Foundation for Inner Peace (www.acim.org).

ISBN: 978-0-925776-17-4
1 2 3 4 5—26 25 24 23

Contents

Preface 9
About *A Course in Miracles* 15

PART I

Sundays with Mundy Epistles 17
Life is in the Mind 19
Everyone Makes an Ego 21
Love Your Enemy 23
Nothing Happened 25
Think Honestly ~ Search Sincerely 27
The Metaphysics of Miracles 29
Home is where the heart is 31
What Causes Depression? 33
Never Think That You Can See Sin 35
Miracles Represent Freedom from Fear 37
Hearing Only One Voice 39
The Ego and COVID-19 41
Who Are You? 43
Never Fear—God Is Here 45
I Am as God Created Me 47
Who Walks with Me? 49
Who Pulls the Puppet's Strings? 51
Time, Revelation and Miracles 53
The Course as a Deterrent for Alzheimer's 55
One Brother Is All Brothers 57
Knowing Our Father's Will 60
Wake Up - Get Up - Clean Up
Grow Up - Show Up 63
Maintaining Sanity in an Insane World 65
The Classroom Called Life 67
Health is Inner Peace 69
Escaping Forever Our Self-Made Cell 71

Love Longing for Itself. 73
Above The Battleground 75
Awakening from the Dreaming 78
Thinking Miraculously 81
I Would Be Happier If. 83
Bringing Order Out of Chaos. 85
Stay Safe and Wait: The Cavalry Is Coming 87
God is Lonely? 89
Nothing Happens by Accident 91
Listening to Our Inner Guide. 93
A New Day Dawning. 95
To See What Jesus Saw. 98
Your Immortal Identity 101
Take It Deeper. 104
Living Consistently Naturally, Miraculously 106
Refusing to Accept Ourselves. .108
Generous Out of Self Interest .110
The Practice of Patience. 112
God Cannot Judge 114
Disciplining the Mind 116
What is Temptation? 118
Love Your Story 121
Ain't Gonna Study War No More. 123
I Am Not a Body!?! 125
"Being" Who We Are Meant "To Be" 127
God Is Life 130

Part II
Jon's Poems 133

Part III
Jon's Sayings. 149

A Sunny Morning—May 1957

On the Farm in Missouri

> Immediate Involvement with Mother Nature
> Eternal Connection with Mother Soil
> Lying in the Woods – Touching Earth
> Listening – Talking to Myself
> Standing in the Field
> Bright Sun -- Warming my Exposed Torso
> Occasional White Clouds
> Many May Flowers – Bees Busily Moving
> My Youthful Body set to Run
> For No Apparent Reason – Alive – Alert
> Awake to the Moment
> Everything is Mine – Everything is Okay
> Such Feelings – So Long Ago
> Forgotten – Remembered
> I'm Free – So is Everyone
> Free to be Human
> Here Now
> On a Sunny Morning in May
> On the Farm in Missouri

Preface

*Time is a trick, a sleight of hand, a vast illusion
in which figures come and go as if by magic.
Yet there is a plan behind appearances
that does not change.
The script is written.
When experience will come to end
your doubting has been set.
For we but see the journey
from the point at which it ended,
looking back on it,
imagining we make it once again;
reviewing mentally what has gone by.*
ACIM WORKBOOK-158.4:1-5

Growing up on a farm in Missouri during the 1940s and 50s meant spending a great deal of time outdoors, working in the fields, gardening, caring for and playing with the animals. Daddy did the morning chores but, like all farm boys, it was my job in the evenings, including milking our cow 'Strawberry.' There was so much milk for our family of four that much of it was given to our cats, dogs and pigs. Whenever possible, we would be riding our horses, hunting in the woods, fishing, or swimming in the nearby north fork of the Salt River. Or playing pool in Mongler's garage.

My only sister Ann and I, along with other kids from nearby farms, enjoyed a happy hard-playing, hard-working, something of a Huckleberry Finn, Tom Sawyer lifestyle. The log cabin in which Mark Twain was born in Florida, Missouri sat in the woods a few miles northwest of our farm until, in 1967 a large pavilion was built to house the cabin, a library, gift shop, and museum.

When I was nine, I told my folks that I was going to be a minister and asked to be baptized. As I grew, I felt consistently compelled to explore the beyond, (Why are we here? Where did we come from?) The only place talking about these matters was the church so I got involved, and our mother Milly, who was something of a mystic, lovingly helped out. We went to church every Sunday. She became a deacon in the church, and president of the Women's Society. When I was ten, she gave me a tin hand-crank organ that looks like a church organ, and hung a picture of Jesus titled "The Savior" by Ralph Pallen Coleman on my bedroom wall. When I was thirteen, she gave me an ostrich-leather-skinned bound 'red letter edition' of the King James Version of the Bible with a handy concordance and index. That picture of Jesus today hangs on the wall to the right of my desk, the Bible sits under my office phone, and the organ—which works as well today as it did all those years ago—sits on the bookshelf.

In the fall of 1961 I enrolled as a pre-ministerial student at Culver-Stockton College in Canton, Missouri. Small town and rural Missouri churches could not afford to hire regular ministers, so they would employ retired ministers or pre-ministerial students. These jobs were only given to junior and senior students. I was, however, able to replace a junior student who dropped out of the program when I was a freshman. I thus stepped into the pulpit of Hawk Point Community Church as their minister in December 1961. I was eighteen and 'licensed,' not ordained, by the Christian Church (Disciples of Christ).

Nearly every Sunday for the next 60 years, I would be in a pulpit somewhere on a Sunday morning, sharing what I hoped others would find to be meaningful and inspirational. Preaching is a great job, as it forces you think things through on an ongoing weekly basis. I completed my Master's in Theology degree at Southern California School of Theology in May 1967 and moved to New York City to begin doctoral studies at the progressive New School University in Greenwich Village. I soon secured a position as minister of Windsor Terrace Community Church in Brooklyn.

The late 60's and early 70's saw the Dawning of the Age of Aquarius. The music of the Beatles, the Rolling Stones and the Doors was forever in the air as was the sweet smell of incense issuing from the brownstone houses in the Village. The musicals "Hair" and "Jesus Christ Superstar" opened on Broadway. And, of course, there was Woodstock. The New School was open to receiving course proposals, so I sent in an application to start teaching classes on Esoteric and Mystical Philosophies, Consciousness Expansion and Religious Experiences—and the like. To my joy and surprise, they said, "Go for it." And I did, with two or three classes per semester for the next ten years.

Always interested in yoga, in August of 1970 I attended a month-long intensive yoga teacher training program in Val Morin Canada led by Swami Vishnu Devananda, which culminated with participation in a fire-walking program. Intrigued by Eastern Philosophy, in 1971 I took off for India, hoping I could find a living master. There I studied with three brilliant teachers—but I could not get into "guru-worship," and returned to New York both inspired and discouraged.

In April 1973 I met Drs. Helen Schucman, the scribe of *A Course in Miracles,* and William Thetford, who attended a talk I gave on 'Consciousness Expansion' at a conference sponsored by Spiritual Frontiers Fellowship. Two years later—in April 1975—Helen and Bill decided it was time to 'formally' introduce me to the manuscript they had been working on, which they did in Dr. Kenneth Wapnick's apartment in New York City. This manuscript was soon to be published by the Foundation for Inner Peace as "A Course in Miracles," now referred to as ACIM and "the Course"

I loved being a minister. I enjoyed helping the older folk, hospital visit, funerals—yes funerals—and wedding and of course preaching. Slowly, slowly, however, I felt a disconnect with traditional Christian theology, especially the emphasis on Jesus suffering and dying 'for our sins.' In 1972 I taught a class on Esoteric Philosophy including a section on the Kabbalah. I invited Rabbi Joseph Gelberman to help me in this endeavor. We soon became friends, and in 1980 he asked me to help him put together The New Seminary—now All Faith Seminary.

After 28 years of working as a Protestant minister it came time to step away from the United Methodist Church. The roots of tradition run deep, and it was clear that my interest in *A Course in Miracles* was not finding welcome in a traditional church setting. In the fall of 1989, Rev. Diane Berke and I founded Interfaith Fellowship, starting in the basement of The Little Synagogue in Greenwich Village, then from 1993-2003 in Cami Hall, a piano recital hall directly across from Carnegie Hall.

My first two books *Awaken to Your Own Call* and *Listening to Your Inner Guide* were published during the mid-90s and, as invitations to speak in other churches began to come in, I gradually stepped off the stage in New York City to spend eighteen years (2002-2020) on the road as a 'guest minister' traveling throughout the United States, Canada and England, working primarily with Unity and Religious Science Churches. In March 2020 Covid brought everything to a screeching halt and everything went Zoom.

Accustomed to writing an inspirational piece for Sunday mornings, my assistant Eileen Katzmann, encouraged me to continue the process by composing weekly "Sunday with Mundy" epistles to be sent out on Sunday mornings. I also began bi-weekly "Sunday with Mundy Live" online podcast discussions with a variety of teachers in spirituality, *A Course in Miracles*, mysticism, near-death experiences, metaphysics—and more. This book is a compilation of fifty-two of these little epistles—one for each week of the year—along with some previously unpublished poems and 'sayings' lifted from a variety of presentations.

We Become What We Think About

Sermon writing, preaching, and teaching has been a godsend. What a blessing it is to 'have to' sit down once a week and put your ideas together in such a way that you could share them with others who will hopefully find what you had to share worthwhile, thought-provoking, and inspirational. The process includes lots of reading, researching, contemplating, writing, listening, sharing, and then starting all over again for the next week, hopefully going even deeper than before. It's not just enough, for example, to talk about forgiveness. It's important to go deeper into understanding how forgiveness heals.

In 1981, I wrote an article titled "Sermon Writing and Preaching as a Process of Individuation" for Preaching Magazine. Individuation as described by psychologist Dr. Carl Jung calls for us to dig deeper... down past the surface traits of the ego and narcissistic self-absorption to the Psyche of humankind—the Soul, the true Self—the Christ in everyone. Could anything be more fun? Are we not always looking for fulfillment and meaning in life? Are we not here to live as best we can a life that is 'on purpose' and fulfilling?

I have a framed inscription on the wall in my office which I found in an antique store in Missour. There is no author. The word "Study" appears at the top in big letters, and below it we read:

Study

The whole Universe is your Library
Authors, Conversations and Remarks
upon them, are your best Tutors.

There is not a wider difference
between Man and Beast
than between Man and Man
And to what is this Difference owing,
But to the Distinguished Improvement
of the Mind by Study and Meditation.

Studying is a healthful, helpful process—and practice. The more we study, the more comfortable and automatic the process of "learning" becomes, analogous to what mathematicians feel in figuring out a complex problem... psychologists feel in understanding the mind, musicians feel when they perfect their art... artists feel when engaging in their craft... gardeners feels in beautifying their gardens... dancers experiences in becoming more proficient in dance... tennis players or any sport players feel as they becomes skilled in their endeavors, or what mothers and fathers feel when they're givers and receivers of love to and from a child.

Remember that no one is where he is by accident,
and chance plays no part in God's plan.
There is, however, no set pattern,
since training is always highly individualized.
ACIM MANUAL-9.1.3&5

Looking back, we see that the lessons we learned along the way were what they were supposed to be, even—or especially—those crashes and burns, the rough spots and bumps that came our way. Though this journey has not always been easy, it's been the right road. Indeed, I have always found that when life took me on a detour, (leaving the church for example), the detour was the right road. According to the Course, time itself—'the story'—is a dream.

The good news is:

> *Happy dreams come true,*
> *not because they are dreams,*
> *but only because they are happy.*
> *And so, they must be loving.*
> *Their message is, "Thy Will be done,"*
> *and not, "I want it otherwise."*
>
> ACIM TEXT-18.V.4:1-3

About *A Course in Miracles*

This is a course in miracles. It is a required course. Only the time you take it is voluntary. Free will does not mean that you can establish the curriculum. It means only that you can elect what you want to take at a given time. The course does not aim at teaching the meaning of love, for that is beyond what can be taught. It does aim, however, at removing the blocks to the awareness of love's presence, which is your natural inheritance. The opposite of love is fear, but what is all-encompassing can have no opposite.
ACIM INTRODUCTION

A Course in Miracles "the Course" is the wisest, sanest, deepest document I know. It is eloquent in its loveliness and level of psychological sophistication.

The Course was scribed—'taken down'—by Helen Schucman, Ph.D., a clinical and research psychologist, who held the tenured position of Associate Professor of Medical Psychology at the College of Physicians and Surgeons at the Columbia-Presbyterian Medical Center in New York City, in conjunction with William Thetford, Ph.D. who was a tenured Professor of Medical Psychology at Columbia University's College of Physicians and Surgeons, and Director of the Psychology Department at the Presbyterian Hospital in New York City for whom Dr. Schucman worked. As her trusted friend and colleague, Dr. Thetford assisted and supported Dr. Schucman throughout the Course's scribing. It was published on June 26, 1976.

The Course contains no dogma, doctrine, no creed, no rules, no regulations, and no required ways of believing. What is unique about the Course is that it brings modern 'psychology' to traditional 'theology,' making it clear which decisions are most beneficial to us and which ones inhibit our growth. Pick up the Course, read just a few pages and you will soon ask, "who wrote this?" It is soon clear that no "body" wrote it. While it came our way through the heart, head, and hands of Helen Schucman, she never thought of herself as the author. She simply wrote down what she heard. The Course was given to us by Jesus, which may sound incredulous to some, but it soon becomes clear that it could be no one else. Who else could say, "I could not have said, "Betrayest thou the Son of man with a kiss?" unless I believed in betrayal." ACIM T-6.I.15:5

The Course takes us deep into an understanding of the metaphysical nature of reality, assuring us that despite the many beautiful aspects of this world, this is also an insane world and is not our eternal home. Heaven—our eternal home—transcends what our body's eyes can see. One of the most important distinctions in the Course is between 'form' and 'content.' Put simply, there are no streets, no cars, no stores, and no artificial lights in Heaven. Heaven is not a place or a condition. Heaven, says the Course,

> *. . . is merely an awareness of perfect Oneness,*
> *and the knowledge that there is nothing else;*
> *nothing outside this Oneness, and nothing else within.*
> ACIM TEXT-18.VI.1:6

PART I

Sundays with Mundy Epistles

Epistle 1

Life is in the Mind

*Nothing is accomplished through death,
because death is nothing.
Everything is accomplished through life,
and life is of the mind and in the mind.
The body neither lives nor dies,
because it cannot contain you who are life.*
ACIM TEXT-6.A.1:2-4

My wife Dolores and I had our Johnson and Johnson Covid shots in March of 2021. Four months later, in July, I contracted Babesiosis, an infection of the red blood cells, caused by a tick bite and a microscopic parasite called Babesia which invades and reproduces in the cell. That sent me to the hospital. My immune system weakened while I was in the hospital, I caught the Delta brand of Covid. I then spent 24 days, alone in a sealed room which I could not leave, and only certain people dressed in protective gear could enter. Every adult should be shut away from the world like this every so often—to 'shut down' the world and provided a chance to turn within. There was plenty of time to meditate and ask once again the same questions I asked as I did as a kid on a farm: What's it all about? How did we get into this world? And who is asking these questions?

In the middle of all that, during the weakest, sickest, darkest night, there came an opportunity to look at death. Death was looking like an attractive option. Many a soldier lying wounded on a battlefield, or anyone very sick for any reason, might easily say, "Yes," to death to be free of the burden of a painful body. Lying there in the dark an inner voice said.

"Go or stay, either way, you will not lose your mind."

Teaching and learning are your greatest strengths now, because they enable you to change your mind and help others to change theirs. —ACIM TEXT-4.I.4:1

Looking at the prospect of bodily death. I chose to hang out in the body for a little longer, for one primary reason—to be with Dolores, our daughter Sarah, and our three grandchildren. Beyond that, there remains learning and living ever more deeply. The Course is here to help us remove 'all' the blocks to the awareness of love's presence. In this sense, it is uncompromising. It is taking us all the way home.

The Course compels us to be the love we are and do the thing we want to do more than anything else, by being present to ourselves and for each other. Lying in the hospital bed, listening to the Course on my cell phone, it was clear that there is even more letting go to do, and one needs simply to allow for "Thy Will to Be Done." God's Will is not different from our will when it is the "right use of will."

The deeper we go, the more we let go,
the more meaning and purpose become clear.

When your body and your ego and your dreams are gone, you will know that you will last forever. Perhaps you think this is accomplished through death, but nothing is accomplished through death, because death is nothing. —ACIM TEXT-6.V.A.1:1-2

Epistle 2

Everyone Makes an Ego

Everyone makes an ego or a self for themself
which is subject to enormous variation because of its instability.
He also makes an ego for everyone else he perceives,
which is equally variable.
Their interaction is a process that alters both,
because they were not made by or with the Unalterable.
T-4.II.2:1-3

One of the 'new to the Course' students, in our ongoing online Zoom class, asked me to be more specific as to what the ego is, as she said, "The ego is not all bad." To which I responded, "No it is not all bad. It is also not all good, and we are looking for that which "is" all good. The ego is the questioning aspect of the post-separation self, which was 'made' rather than 'created.' The ego is a wrong-minded attempt to see ourselves as we would like to be, rather than who we are. The ego would have us see ourselves as 'special,' smarter, stronger, richer, prettier perhaps, with a body that is more handsome than the average. The ego is something that is "made up" i.e., imagined, as is the world in which we live, i.e., projection 'makes' perception.

It is our desire to be completely free of the split mind and to bring to the mind only the awareness of the truth of our being as pure Spirit. More specifically, this thing we call "an ego" simply does not exist. God knows us as he created us, not as we have created ourselves. The ego is simply a belief in a separated or false self that we make up as a substitute for the Self that God created.

Why are you unhappy?
Because 99.9% of everything you think and say and do,
is about yourself. And there isn't one.
Terence Gray aka Wei Wu Wei (1895-1986)

Since the ego is nothing more than a dream, it then becomes a "block to the awareness of love's presence." The Course helps us engage in a process of awakening from the sleepy, recalcitrant and unconscious ego to an awareness of our reality as Children of God. It is a slow and gradual process that introduces us to our eternal reality.

God created each of us in Love, and Love remains forever the core of our being. Polishing over this wonderful gift of God, the ego asserts itself as something separate from God, capable of making up its own world, which it then seeks to do. This happens in every dimension of life: family life, in schools, in the workplace, and in positions of political power. A minister friend tells the story of a church he served where the chairman of the board (a retired naval officer) essentially ran the church, making sure everything was 'ship shape' and making it impossible for my friend to effectively carry out his ministry. Eventually, with the blessing of the naval officer, he had to quit.

We see egos acting out repeatedly on the world's stage – with full-size, aggressive egos, would-be tyrants and demagogues, willing to engage in deceitful practices in order to be A#1, King of the Hill, Top of the Heap. It is a sad story told over and over again in the history of this world. It was a favorite theme revealed in Shakespeare's tragedies and thousands of other sad stories.

The Course is a guidebook to helping us ferret out this made-up self so that we might then discover and therefore recover the Truth of our Being, which is buried in a world of fantasy and make-believe. The Seeker begins this process of Self-discovery by looking deep within, identifying impurities in the psychic system, and exposing them to the light, which with forgiving eyes shines insanity away. This, God, does for everyone when we willingly join him in the exciting discovery of our Self our Soul, our Spirit.

You could say "Well God is an idea too, just like the ego." And you would be correct. The difference is that God is eternal Reality, while the ego is a temporal construct. The Course tells us in the first paragraph that "the opposite of love is fear but what is all-encompassing can have no opposite." Simply put, it is impossible to be separated from the 'wholeness of the self,' or 'spirit,' which is changeless and eternal. Nothing can be antithetical to God. As we come know to more of God, of Love, the more we come to know ourselves.

Say with me:
There is no cruelty in God, and none in me.

Epistle 3

Love Your Enemy

Anger cannot occur
unless you believe that
you have been attacked,
that your attack is justified in return,
and that you are in no way responsible for it.
Given these three wholly irrational premises,
the equally irrational conclusion that a brother is
worthy of attack rather than of love must follow.
ACIM TEXT-6.IN.1:3-4

To summarize *A Course in Miracles* in a few words I would say, "*Do not judge. Do not attack. Do not defend* (your ego) *and do not hide*—that is lie." Both *A Course in Miracles* and *A Course in Love* say this world is a classroom. In fact, every mystical, metaphysical, spiritual tradition I know, says this world is a school. Sometimes, it may seem like a psychiatric institution, a hospital or reformatory. We're here to learn something, otherwise we would not be here. The good news is that: *Learning itself, like the classrooms in which it occurs, is temporary.* It is possible to complete the assignment we've given ourselves, graduate and go home and we don't have to die to go home. Enlightenment, after all, *is but a recognition, not a change at all.* —T-2.II.5:3

It's important not to attack insanity—that only complicates the matter. That does nothing to heal the world or ourselves. As Jesus expresses it in the gospels "You have heard it said, 'Love your neighbor and hate your enemy,' but I tell you, love your enemies and pray for those who persecute you, that you may be children of your Father in Heaven." The insanity of the world can only stop—inside me and inside you.

Salvation asks but a little wish that what is true be true;
a little willingness to overlook what is not there;
a little sigh that speaks for Heaven as a preference to
this world that death and desolation seem to rule.
ACIM TEXT-26.VII.10:1

23

SUNDAYS WITH MUNDY

It's a matter of dropping all attack thoughts, all defenses and letting love instead of anger and attack rule the day. Jesus did it and so can we. The next time a temptation comes up to attack anyone, any concept, any aberrant behavior in any way. Stop! Look at it. Let it go. Look at the silly ego and remember,

Nothing real can be threatened.
Nothing unreal exists.
Herein lies the peace of God.
ACIM TEXT-IN.2:2-4

Epistle 4

Nothing Happened

We cannot speak nor write nor even think of this at all.
It comes to every mind when total recognition that its will
is God's has been completely given and received completely.
It returns the mind into the endless present,
where the past and future cannot be conceived.
It lies beyond salvation; past all thought of time,
forgiveness and the holy face of Christ.
The Son of God has merely disappeared
into his Father, as his Father has in him.
The world has never been at all.
Eternity remains a constant state.
ACIM WORKBOOK-169.6:1-7

I received an email from a student asking, "Why was the separation needed?" I answered simply saying that it was not needed, and, in fact, it never even happened. What? Sometimes the metaphysics of the Course makes you do a double-take; but, if you let the intuitive mind grasp it, you can see that what at first appears absurd is in fact true. Not only was the separation not needed, but it also never happened because it is not possible to be separated from the Mind of God. Or, you could say that it happened in time; but seeing how there is no time, again, it never happened.

Atonement corrects illusions, not truth.
Therefore, it corrects what never was.
The Will of God is entirely apart from time.
So is all reality, being of Him.
The instant the idea of separation
entered the mind of God's Son,
in that same instant was God's Answer given.
In time this happened very long ago.
In reality it never happened at all.
ACIM MANUAL 2.2:2-8

The ego lives in time and is defined by time. It has a past, a present, and a future. For the Self you are in truth, there is no time, no place, and no state where God is not. God cannot separate Himself from Himself; and, as you are part of God, there cannot be any separation from Yourself. Enlightenment is simply a recognition. It is not a change at all. Our night-time dreams may seem quite real while we are having a dream. Yet, we awake in the morning to what we call reality, and we recognize that what happened within the context of our dream never occurred.

Psychologists tell us that the average person goes through eight dream cycles per night; and there can be many dreams within a dream cycle, as dreams tend to morph from one form into another form. For example, you are on a bus; but no, it is a train; no, it is an airplane. There are now over eight billion people on this planet. Each one is having eight dream cycles per night. That equals over 64 billion dreams per night, and something like 99.9% of these dreams are not remembered.

All we see or seem is but a dream within a dream.
EDGAR ALLAN POE (1809-1849)

Our night-time dreams and our daytime dreams have a different form. That is all. Who we are in truth has nothing to do with what we are dreaming. We are now, always have been, and always will be a perfect part of the Mind of God. That is all that matters, and that is all that is real.

If you are as God created you,
then there has been no separation of your mind from His,
no split between your mind and other minds,
and only unity within your own.
ACIM WORKBOOK-110.4:2

Epistle 5

Think Honestly ~ Search Sincerely

*Think honestly what you have thought
that God would not have thought, and what you have
not thought that God would have you think?
Search sincerely for what you have done and left undone
accordingly, and then change your mind to think with God's.*
ACIM TEXT-4.IV.2:4-5

An anonymous, relatively new student of the Course writes,
"How come the Course in Miracles is so negative?
Is that any way to teach a good thing?"

* * * * *

"This is not a course in Creating the Positive
It is a course in Removing the Negative."
KEN WAPNICK

The Course is about *removing the blocks to the awareness of love's presence*. It is not about "adding" anything as everyone already has everything. The Course asks us to look at our fears, in order that we might find freedom from them.

Only the Shadow Knows

The darkness that lurks within, Dr. Carl Jung called the shadow. We experience the shadow in behaviors that are "out of character." Anger, attack, anxiety, all the addictions [over-eating, alcoholism, drugs and more], depression, laziness, and self-indulgence are a few of the many manifestations of the shadow. We see the shadow in things we do not want to acknowledge about ourselves though we see them easily in others.

The Course asks us to *"Think Honestly."* Mark Twain once said that nothing was quite as satisfying as the failure of a friend. He could be incredibly irreverent. He could also call a thing the way it might be seen from a strikingly honest perspective. Did you ever experience jealousy upon hearing of a friend's success? Have you ever felt good about hearing of the misfortune of someone you did not like?

The ego/shadow lives in the basement, surfacing when we over-spend, over-eat, brag, dominate a conversation or overdo most anything. The more we don't look inside, the more we may fall into anxiety, depression—even insanity. Dr. Carl Jung describes how in therapy one day, a 45-year-old patient blurted out: "But I could never admit that I wasted the last 25 years of my life!"

Underneath it all we love each other but *projection makes perception*, and the ego easily covers things over with the grievances it holds against the world. If I project my problems on to the world, I don't have to look inside to find out what is going on. The only way to remove the blocks to an awareness of love's presence is by looking at the blocks. In Christian mysticism one finds freedom from the devil by calling the devil by name. Of course, the devil is not real and "demon rum" can have no power over anyone unless "we" give it that power.

We cannot remove a block—like unforgiveness—unless we look to see what the block is. We look at the shadow, not to confirm its existence, rather do we look at it, in order to dispel its power. Letting go of the negative, that which is true comes to the fore. God is Life. God is Love. Life is Love and Love is Life.

Epistle 6

The Metaphysics of Miracles

The more I study physics.
The more I'm drawn to metaphysics.
ALBERT EINSTEIN

Ken Wapnick used to say, "You can't go far in learning the Course without understanding the basic metaphysics of the Course." As physics deals with the material world, so metaphysics focuses on the mind and the way the mind constructs reality. According to material philosophy, matter is the fundamental substance in nature, and all things, including mental states, evolve from material interaction.

According to non-dual philosophy and the Course, to say, "In the beginning God," is to say that, in the beginning we have Mind. Mind precedes and transcends time and space. Mind is not limited to this world. The Big Bang might be seen as the first split into form. It's where time begins; and with that we have split, split, split, into a Googleplex of unending variations. What we have then is "God," "Being," or pure mind, and a split off into "divided minds." The Course teaches thus:

Whatever you accept into your mind has reality for you.
It is your acceptance of it that makes it real.
If you enthrone the ego in your mind,
your allowing it to enter makes it your reality.
This is because the mind is capable of creating reality
or making illusions.
ACIM TEXT-5.V.4:1-4

Ego constructs of perceived reality are not reality. They are forms of dreaming. We are trying to make a leap from constructing reality to knowing reality as it is. Dropping all preconceptions may seem like a tall order, but there is nothing that says we cannot progressively move in this direction.

One of the main teachings from Ken Wapnick came in his suggestion that we should just be normal. Do what regular people do. Find a way to earn a living doing something you enjoy, have friends, raise a family if you wish, and along the way deepen your relationship with Our Father in Heaven. In the meantime, refrain from judging the world and the people in it. To judge is not to know. Everyone we meet is a brother or a sister; and insofar as that is true, our task is one of loving each other, as only the Christ in you can do.

Ultimately, our will and God's Will are one and the same. That is not, of course, our everyday experience. Fortunately, the memory of God's Will remains in every mind. We get in touch with that memory as we fall in love with the whole of Life. No matter how difficult the lesson that comes our way. Do not curse it. Bless it and see what blessing it can bring to you. In Lesson 253, *My Self is the ruler of the universe*, we read:

It is impossible that anything
should come to me unbidden by myself.
Even in this world, it is I who rule my destiny.
What happens is what I desire.
What does not occur I do not want to happen.
ACIM WORKBOOK-1:1-4

In my struggle with Covid and Babesiosis, I came to understand that I had to love these two diseases and see what gifts they brought my way. There was a reason they were here, and in appreciation of their gifts, I looked to see if I could transcend the thought that what was happening was wrong or bad or should not have happened. It was what it was, and in that, there came a healing of the body and the mind.

Epistle 7

Home is where the heart is
We are always headed Home

Your home has called to you since time began,
nor have you ever failed entirely to hear.
ACIM TEXT-20.II.8:5&9

A Valentine Story

At one of our Tuesday evening online ACIM Zoom classes folks were sharing stories about times in their lives when they "actually thought" they heard a voice. In one of my earlier books, *Listening to Your Inner Guide*, I listed several "messages" folks told me they had heard. They were all very short comforting phrases. Judith Fuller, one of the members of our online class told me the following story.

"I want to share a time when I heard an audible (comforting) voice. It was in 1992, the very first time my husband kissed me (in a car behind a Krystal Burger place... how romantic, huh?). He leaned over and kissed me, and I heard a very audible, firm, full voice say, 'HOME.' It was quite startling. I had to check to be sure it wasn't someone nearby talking to me. But it has proven to be true. In this life, on this path, wherever he goes, I am home."

Another short story

I was the minister of Windsor Terrace Community Church in Brooklyn, NY from 1968-1978. There was an older member of the church, a shut-in named Mrs. Voight. As she could not come to church, I would make regular calls to her home. Mrs. Voight had a full-time live-in housekeeper/nurse. On several occasions, the nurse called me saying she thought Mrs. Voight was dying. I would go, but Mrs. Voight would not die.

Finally, the day came when the nurse called and said she thought Mrs. Voight really was dying and I should come. I went and, indeed, Mrs. Voight was dying. As the nurse and I stood by her bed, Mrs. Voight began to cry, saying, "I want to go Home! I want to go Home!" And the nurse said, "*Now nonsense Mrs. Voight, you are home.*" Meaning, she was in her apartment in Brooklyn. When the nurse did that, I asked her if she would leave us alone as I wanted to say some prayers with Mrs. Voight.

The second the bedroom door closed; Mrs. Voight opened her eyes which had been closed all this time. She said nothing but looked at me with a kind of "Help me" look on her face. I looked at her and said, "Mrs. Voight you can go home whenever you want to." Tears started running down her cheeks. She looked at me. She said, "Thank you!" She closed her eyes and before the day was over, she went Home.

Years later when I told this story at a workshop at Unity of Syracuse NY, Cybie Mauro, a workshop participant, told a nearly identical story. Cybie and her sisters were all in her mother's bedroom when Cybie's mother also started saying, "I want to go Home!" And when, just like Mrs. Voight's nurse, one of Cybie's sisters pointed out to her that she was in her home, her mother exclaimed, "No, not this home!"

Where does Dorothy want to go in *The Wizard of Oz*? Home. Where does Alice in *Alice in Wonderland* want to go? Home. Where does the boy in the modern fairy tale *The Polar Express* want to go? Home. Where is Dorothy? Where is Alice? Where is the boy in The Polar Express story? They are all home safely tucked in their beds. They were only dreaming.

Where are you? Where do you want to go?

Home is where the heart is. We never left home. We've only been dreaming.

Epistle 8

What Causes Depression?

Out of curiosity, I typed "Causes of Depression" into the Google search engine. It led to an article in "Psychology Today" magazine which listed eight reasons for depression. They were—winter weather; smoking; thyroid deficiencies; poor sleep; social media; noise pollution; lack of Omega-3; and too much TV.

All these "causes for depression" suggest that the reason for unhappiness and despair is due to something coming from the outside. According to the Course, the cause of depression cannot be related to anything external—unless "we think it is." Depression rather comes from our having *forsworn* God. To *forswear* means to abandon or reject. To forswear God means to fail in our responsibility to ourselves as children of God.

You are not at peace because you are not fulfilling your function.
God gave you a very lofty function that you are not meeting.
ACIM TEXT-4.I.9:4

We are here to love one another and hereby heal all the hurts the fearful ego would cast upon us. Depression is only tangentially related to things like weather, noise pollution, thyroid deficiencies, poor sleep, or too much TV. Lesson 65 from the Course is, "My only function is the one God gave me." The problem is that we have chosen wrongly. We have been listening to the ego and ignoring God. We have not been forgiving. We have not been loving. Jesus is simply someone who made "the" right choices with consistence and thereby remembered God. We cannot earn God's love. How could you earn what you already have? As principle 29 from the 50 Miracle principles tells us.

Miracles praise God through you.
They praise Him by honoring His creations,
affirming their perfection.
They heal because they deny body-identification
and affirm spirit-identification.
ACIM TEXT-1.1:29

The demonstration of simple kindness can be very helpful in lifting our spirits. Peace is stronger than war and nothing is stronger than gentleness. Kindness like an ever-flowing stream, can wear away the roughest edges. Loving-kindness and gentleness are stronger than anger and attack. Bullies and tyrants melt in the presence of loving-kindness! If you want to get out of depression, as the old song sung by Jimmy Durante said it, "make someone happy, make just one someone happy and you will be happy too."

I came across the following quote when I was 18. I loved it so much I wrote it down, stuck in on the wall next to my bathroom mirror and put it to memory. Maybe you would like to do the same.

I shall pass through this world but once.
Any good therefore that I can do,
or any kindness that I can show
to any human being let me do it now.
Let me not defer nor neglect it
for I shall not pass this way again.
French-born American Quaker
Stephen Grellet (1773–1855)

Or maybe repeat the following from the Course:

Holiness created me holy
Kindness created me kind.
Helpfulness created me helpful
Perfection created me perfect.
ACIM WORKBOOK-67.2:3

Epistle 9

Never Think That You Can See Sin

Every once in a while, you will find a "knock your socks" off sentence in the Course that seems extra strong, and you know it is 100% right. Such is the case in the following sentences from the *Song of Prayer*, a booklet received by Helen Schucman after the Course was completed and the last thing she wrote.

As prayer is always for yourself,
so is forgiveness always given you.
It is impossible to forgive another,
for it is only your sins you see in him.
You want to see them there, and not in you.
That is why forgiveness of another is an illusion.
Yet it is the only happy dream in all the world.
the only one that does not lead to death.
Only in someone else can you forgive yourself,
for you have called him guilty of your sins,
and in him must your innocence now be found.
Who but the sinful need to be forgiven?
And do not ever think you can see sin
in anyone except yourself.
ACIM The Song of Prayer 21:4

God does not forgive sin. God being Love does not condemn. No forgiveness is called for if there is no condemnation. You have already been forgiven all your sins, so has everyone. God knows nothing of retribution. Likewise, God has no favorite children, as everyone is equally loved. We cannot see sin in anyone unless sin is first found within.

Back in the 1970s during the infamous Watergate hearings, it became common to demonize Richard Nixon in cartoons and skits. A friend tells the story of being all anti-Nixon when something happened which he could not have predicted. Nixon's wife Pat passed away, and the funeral was broadcast on live television. He said he saw Richard Nixon—and he was in tears, absolutely broken up. My friend said:

"I realized then that the villain was not him—it was me
and my judgment—and I only felt compassion for
the man moving forward. Never again did I hate him."

Accept each day whatever life throws your way.
Remember this world is a school,
and we choose our own curriculum.
There is no one to blame
not the Republicans or the Democrats,
the Catholics or the Protestants.
The blacks, the whites or the Jews.
There is no running away from this thing called life.
Suicide is not a solution.
Drugs and alcohol solve nothing at all.
Face each day straight on shoulders back.
Do not blame anyone for anything.
With a little luck you'll see Heaven is here and now.
It is not a place nor a condition.
it is merely an awareness of Perfect Oneness.

Epistle 10

Miracles Represent Freedom from Fear

How is your fear/love level? Who rules your heart, your head your home? Are you able to maintain your balance, your peace of mind and stability when others seem to be losing theirs? One of the things I say repeatedly is:

"Don't let anything take the peace of God away from you."

Principle 26 of the 50 Miracle Principles tells us

Miracles represent freedom from fear.
"Atoning" means "undoing." The undoing of fear
is an essential part of the Atonement value of miracles.

We all have split or divided minds. A part of our mind is ruled by the ego, which by its very nature is fearful. It comes knocking on our door bringing us illusory toys—distress, depression, attack, anger, war and disease. The other part, the soft gentle voice of the Holy Spirit reminds us of our eternal home where love, health and truth abide. Who will you listen to today, the ego with its fearful dramas being played out in the mind and in the world or will the Holy Spirit be your guide enabling your equilibrium?

Fear is a stranger to the ways of love.
Identify with fear,
and you will be a stranger to yourself.
And thus, you are unknown to you.
ACIM WORKBOOK-160.1:1-3

The ego is fear based because, deep inside it knows, its days are numbered. Someday, it will lose its hold on the mind. In the meantime, the more we identify with the ego, the more off balance, anxious and stressed out we become, the more we are open ourselves to dis-ease. Much of what happened in the stock market crash of October 1929 could have been prevented if reason had ruled the day. It was, as we all know, a preface to the Great Depression.

Both *A Course in Miracles* and *A Course of Love* tell us that the body is an instrument, a tool, a mechanism, and a communication device. As long as we "seem" to occupy a body, we want to keep that instrument working well. Obviously, the greater the overall health of any "body" the less stressed out it is, the less likely it is to get even a simple cold even when exposed to germs. Be it the common flu or the coronavirus, flu we know, is most likely to affect those with compromised immune systems.

The Course encourages us to be careful—watch and let all fearful thoughts go . . .

> *dancing in the wind, dipping and turning till they disappear, far, far outside of you. And turn you to the stately calm within, where in holy stillness dwells the living God you never left, and Who never left you. The Holy Spirit takes you gently by the hand, and retraces with you your mad journey outside yourself, leading you gently back to the truth and safety within. He brings all your insane projections and the wild substitutions that you have placed outside you to the truth. Thus, He reverses the course of insanity and restores you to reason.* —ACIM TEXT-18.8:1-5

Let's do the logical, reasonable things that health professionals tell us to do. If you're driving a car do so safely. Take care of that body you move around in, keep it healthy physically and mentally. Watch people on YouTube talk about the practical things that people should do to keep their bodies running well and, in the meantime,

"Don't let anything take the peace of God away from you."

Epistle 11

Hearing Only One Voice

If you cannot hear the Voice for God,
it is because you do not choose to listen.
That you "do" listen to the voice of your ego is demonstrated
by your attitudes, your feelings and your behavior.
ACIM TEXT-4.IV.1:2

A Course in Miracles and A Course of Love are both trying to teach us a new way of thinking, seeing and being. We read in the prelude to *A Course of Love*, "*The teachings you need now are to help you separate the ego from your Self, to help you learn to hear only one voice.*" The ego's voice is insane because it tries to teach us that we are something other than what we are in truth. We're learning how to be more sensitive to "the voice inside our hearts," what *A Course of Love* calls "wholeheartedness." If we can succeed at this, we then wind up with the mystic's point of view: *loving rather than condemning everything we see.* The more respectful and responsible we can be the more we begin to love the face in the mirror, the more we love the whole, the more life simply and beautifully falls into place.

Spirit am I, a holy Son of God, free of all limits, safe and healed and whole, free to forgive, and free to save the world. You are in truth "a holy child of God," and that "Identity is so secure, so lofty, sinless, glorious and great, wholly beneficent and free from guilt, that Heaven looks to It to give it light."
ACIM WORKBOOK-244.1:1

Is this Helpful or Hurtful?

Principle No. 5 from the *50 Miracle Principles* says, "*Miracles are habits and should be involuntary.*" Hurtful habits often 'seem' involuntary. I say, 'seem' involuntary as 'all' actions are backed up by first being a decision. It's helpful to pay attention to how often some judgmental statement comes pouring forth from the lips. Is this the way the Holy Spirit would speak to you? I listened to Dr. David Perlmutter's book *Brain Wash*. He describes a very unpretentious

39

principle which says simply, *the more you do something, the more you will do it.* That sounds simplistic. It is simplistic. It is also true. Look at any repetitive activity and ask, "is this helpful or hurtful?" And remember:

If you attack error in another, you will hurt yourself.
ACIM TEXT-3.III.7:1

We need mind training simply because as the Course says, our minds are *totally undisciplined* (W-20.2:6). Doing the work of the Course we more clearly learn how to think in alignment with loving inner guidance. This guidance "lifts us up." Guidance from the ego, literally, "pulls us down" leading us to believe we are something other than what we are in truth.

Being uplifted is the very opposite of depression. We are looking to "breed out of ourselves" a certain kind of negativity—a way of looking down on the world and ourselves which is hurtful to ourselves and to those on whom our negativity is poured. We then open the door to a greater degree of loving kindness—everyone feels better, and we bring a little ray of light into the world. Remember, the voice we hear is the voice we replicate. It is up to us to choose which voice we will listen to, which command we will follow. As we give, so do we receive.

Epistle 12

The Ego and COVID-19

Digging Deeper—Going Within

There is something about the experience of the Coronavirus that could help us understand more clearly the non-reality of the ego. Neither the ego nor the coronavirus are living entities. We often talk about the ego as though it is a real thing, as in, "The devil made me do it." Or "The ego made me do it." The ego is a fantasy, an illusion, an "idea" only. It is something that we have made up, and now it "seems as though" it is real. There are no egos in Heaven. The Holy Spirit does not recognize the ego or dialogue with the ego. If the Holy Spirit did, it would mean that the ego was a real thing.

Back in the 1980's, Sir Alister Hardy, a professor at Oxford University, did a study of 5,000 descriptions of mystical experiences. Surprisingly, he found that the major stimulant to an awakening in mystical awareness was despair and depression leading to a "crash and burn" experience, followed by a release of the ego mind, and then the often-overwhelming experience of Love's Presence.

The second most likely stimulant Dr. Hardy found was exactly the opposite of *crashing and burning*: namely, *meditation and contemplation*, getting quiet and going within. What happens in either case is the ultimate release of ego control. Our major problem, the Course says, is "The Authority Problem." We say to God—"Thank you very much, God, but I would rather do it myself." This never works. No matter how much success we might achieve in life, without God, we are left with the feeling that something is missing. What is missing is an awareness of the Spirit that gives us life in the first place. Only by giving up on the ego's plan and learning to follow what the Course calls "God's Plan for Salvation" do we find peace, freedom, and salvation.

In a Washington Post article titled "The Corona Virus isn't Alive," we read: "*Outside a host, viruses are dormant. They have none of the traditional trappings of life: metabolism, motion, the ability to reproduce.*" My friend Dr. Rod Chelberg, M.D, explains it this way.

The Coronavirus is more like a malicious computer virus than a living thing. Just like a virus, the ego's way of thinking has been downloaded into our minds, and there it has begun to replicate itself.

We human beings follow "ego programs" given to us by our society, our religion, our parents, their parents, and so on. It's not done with any malicious intent; it's just the way this world has been running for many thousands of years. As it says in the song from the musical *South Pacific*: "You have to be taught to hate and fear. You have to be carefully taught."

The Coronavirus is not a living thing. Likewise, the ego is not a living thing. It is a an "idea." It is a "program." However, we can't get free of the program unless we realize we have been infected by it. Then, giving up on the ego's program of fear and hate, we find a much more pleasant song to which we can listen. It comes from God Himself, via "The Holy Spirit." This song is very pleasant, very melodious. It is Heaven's Way: we are here to love each other—there is no fighting. There is no need for attack or anger. Heaven is inside me. It is in you. The love of God is in all of us. Here it will stay. We have just been dreaming. Awakening, we find we have never left Heaven.

Epistle 13

Who Are You?

What you think you are is a belief to be undone.
But what you really are must be revealed to you.
The belief you are a body calls for correction, being a mistake.
The truth of what you are calls on the strength in you
to bring to your awareness what the mistake conceals.
ACIM WORKBOOK-91.6:7-10

The recognition of your own invulnerability
is important to the restoration of your sanity.
ACIM TEXT-12. V.2:1

The Coronavirus draws us up short and calls us to awaken from complacency and unconscious comfortability. It prompts us to remember who we are in truth. There is a line in *The Urantia Book* that says: "*Mortals only learn wisdom by experiencing tribulation.*" Like any disaster, the virus is a slap in the ego's face—challenging the invulnerability of the body. The body is the ego's chosen home, but we are not an ego, and there is no safety in any body. Every "body" disappears—"*ashes to ashes, dust to dust.*" Bodies are *temporal*. Even 90 or 100 years is as nothing in relationship to Eternity. Life in a body lasts only for a moment, and then, as Shakespeare's Hamlet laments:

Out, out, brief candle! Life's but a walking shadow,
a poor player that struts and frets his hour upon the stage
and then is heard no more.
It is a tale told by an idiot, full of sound and fury,
signifying nothing."

When the vulnerability of who we are as a body comes into question, we sit up, look around and say:" Why is this happening? Death is knocking on my neighbor's door. Will he come to visit me as well?" The Course tells us that this world is a dream. Yet, we prefer sleep to being awake, since being awake means being responsible, and being responsible requires my attention and "willingness" to forego fearful dreams in recognition of my true identity in God. This is the only way to lasting contentment and lasting peace.

SUNDAYS WITH MUNDY

Faced with the Coronavirus, we had to shelter in place. We can decide to drink, eat, watch TV, and sleep; or perhaps we can choose to stop and go within, meditate, exercise, read *A Course in Miracles, A Course of Love*—or some other guide to deepening and expanding our awareness. It's a good time to examine our ideas—to try to make sense out of life. What is life? Am I "alive" just because I have a body? Do we "live" for perhaps 90 years and then blank, nothing, emptiness, no mind, no spirit—nada?

The remembrance of love brings invulnerability with it.
ACIM TEXT-10.III.3:3

Every religion in the world says, "God is Love." Is love a thing? Does it have a form? If you try to tell me what Love is, you may have some nice words to share; but is that it? The Course also says, "God is Life." Does life have to have a material form? Does God have a body with lungs that need oxygen?

From the perspective of the body, however, from the first "inhalation" to the last breath, when we "expire," Life "seems to" inhabit a body. Nevertheless, Spirit is forever and always without form and does not need a body. Mind, the Course tells us, is the "*activating agent of spirit*" —ACIM CLARIF-1.1, and "*the mind that serves spirit is invulnerable.*" —ACIM TEXT-1.IV.2:11

Spirit am I, free of all limits, safe and healed and whole, free to forgive, and free to save the world.
ACIM WORKBOOK-97.7:2

Your Life is God's Life. God's Life is Your Life.
Our Life is God's Life, and All Life is One Life.

Epistle 14

Never Fear—God Is Here

I am "your" resurrection and "your" life.
I am the model for rebirth.
Rebirth is merely the dawning on your mind
of what is already in it.
You live in me because you live in God.
Believe in the resurrection
because it has been accomplished,
and it has been accomplished in you.
ACIM TEXT-11.VI.4:6

"I feel a great disturbance in the force.
As though millions of voices cried out."
Obi-wan Kenobi in original Star Wars Trilogy

We who are mortal, are being asked to awaken to a deeper awareness of our immortality. What is happening now involves the entire planet. It's not like, a war in Afghanistan or Iraq or some specific war-torn place. The whole of humanity is being forced to go within. Are you letting this be for you a time for a deepening of awareness of Spirit? Are you able to get quiet, meditate, read, study, reflect or write? There are some folks who have chosen to get lost in the news, others are hiding in the bottom of a bottle or yet some other dreary, dismal place. This time of cloistering ourselves can be an opportunity for looking past the outside to the Kingdom of Heaven within.

I wrote my master's thesis in Theology on "Consciousness Expansion" based on the work of French Jesuit Priest Father Pierre Teilhard de Chardin. Chardin spoke of the development of a noospheric link in consciousness, what he referred to as a world wide web of awareness. He died in 1955, well before the development of personal computers. He was talking about something he saw happening on a "psychic" non-material level of mind

Did you ever lay in bed in the early morning hours—awake but not yet ready to put your feet on the floor? Did you ever lay there

45

and say, "*Help me God*!?" I did that once and I heard a voice, (it was not an audible voice) but it wasn't the ego's voice either. Something said, "*God is here. Never Fear.*" Lesson 49 from *A Course in Miracles* says, "*God's Voice Speaks to me all through the day.*" God's voice does indeed speak to each one of us all the time, every day. The only question is, "Are we tuned in and are we listening?" Sometimes we get slapped in the face by what we call "reality," and then we awaken. It's not that God slaps us. God's voice is very gentle. It's just that sometimes in an unconscious way, both individually and collectively without our conscious awareness, we put ourselves to the test.

A much more peaceful process for awakening is to get quiet. It's usually quiet in the morning and the mind has been at rest. Neurologists tell us that while we sleep our brains get a good "washing." Thus, the early morning hour between awaking and arising is a good time to listen. *Consciousness*, the Course says, *is the receptive mechanism, receiving messages from above or below, from the Holy Spirit or the ego.* C-1.7:3. Before the computer is turned on, before the radio or TV pulls you into "the dreaming of the world;" it's a good time to be receptive. Listen!

Rather than saying, "*Help me God.*" Try saying, "*Dear God, how can I help?*" Then, real help can come. We are called upon to be responsible, to stop all projection, release all judgment, fault-finding, attack, and anger and then do nothing. Extend only love to all brothers and sisters, remembering that—"one brother is all brothers." Be the Child of God that you were meant to be. Just as you cannot hurt another without hurting yourself. In like manner neither can you help another without receiving help.

Epistle 15

I Am as God Created Me

Perfect vision will heal all the mistakes
that any mind has made at any time or place.
ACIM WORKBOOK-110.2.1

I awoke one morning thinking about the Covid-19 virus with several compelling "favorite" maxims going through my mind.

Life can only be lived forward
but it can only be understood backwards.
Danish Theologian Soren Kierkegaard (1813-1855)

When you are going through hell—keep going.
Winston Churchill (1874-1965)

In the middle of every difficulty lies opportunity.
Albert Einstein (1879-1955)

No one is where he is by accident,
and chance plays no part in God's plan.
ACIM MANUAL-9.1:3

No one dies without his own consent.
ACIM WORKBOOK-152.1:4

Sometimes good things fall apart
so better things can fall together.
Marilyn Monroe (1926-1962)

When everything is falling apart,
something else is trying to be born.
The Dali Lama

and,

Everything that seems to happen to me I ask for,
and receive as I have asked.
ACIM TEXT-21.II.2:5

The last of these maxims draws us up short. What? Really? That's rather stark. I asked for this? It is here for a reason and it's here for everyone. Not since an asteroid killed off the dinosaurs some sixty million years ago has the entire planet been so completely engulfed in one catastrophic experience. Within the context of our collective dream, Covid-19 appears as a present reality. This is not God's doing unless you believe in a cruel and unjust God. Yet, it's here for a reason, and for more than one season bring us together in a deeper awareness of collective oneness.

When anything "seems" to come to us as though from the outside, it's a good idea to stop, look and listen. "Why are we going through this?" According to an article in New York Magazine titled "The Good Side of Bad Dreams" sleep researchers say nightmares can be seen as the "release" of bad dreams and a cleaning out of anxieties, buried deep down inside. One always feels better after throwing up and getting the poison out of the system. In the same way "confession" can indeed be good for the soul.

The first step in *A Course in Miracles* comes in "removing the blocks" to an awareness of love's presence. Some "blocks" can be a bit heavy. Others not so bad. Some habits easily abandoned; others more ingrained. We look at the dark side, not to affirm its reality, we look in order to let go of its unreality. The pandemic gives us a bit of a look at the one mind through a somewhat painful door.

Amid a pandemic—don't panic. The word panic comes from the Greek word *Pan,* the god of woods and fields and the source of mysterious sounds which caused animals to be afraid. In all things be sane. Sane comes from the Latin *sanus* meaning to be of *sound health*—also "to be in order." Remain sane amid insanity, even seeing suffering and pain. Build your immunity. Counsel and teach and do what you can. As couples and families spend time together, so relationship can deepen and grow. Some day we will talk about how 2020-21 brought us all together. Read, write, meditate, pray, clean the cabinets, the closets, the garage the yard and the floor. When you get done help the person next door.

Epistle 16

Who Walks with Me?

This question should be asked a thousand times a day,
till certainty has ended doubting and established peace.
Today let doubting cease.
God speaks for you in answering
your question with these words:
"I walk with God in perfect holiness. I light the world,
I light my mind and all the minds
which God created one with me."
ACIM WORKBOOK-156.8:1-5

While our bodies may be separated from other bodies, the Course assures us, we can never be alone because as Lesson 41 tells us, *the Source of all life goes with you wherever you go.*

Every religion in the world has some concept of the Holy Spirit. Tribal religions have always believed in the presence of spirits (life) in rocks, and trees, animals and in each other. The Zoroastrians of ancient Persia spoke of the *Spenta Mainu.* The ancient Greek philosopher Socrates spoke of an *"inner genius,"* inside every mind. The Stoics of ancient Greece and Rome spoke of *"an intelligent principle which pervades the Universe."* In Judaism the Divine Spirit is called *Rauch* (Breath) *Hakodesh* (Holy) and *Shechinah* the indwelling feminine, nurturing aspect of God and source of inspiration.

In the New Testament the Holy Spirit is called the Counselor, Comforter, Healer, Guide, Mediator, and Teacher. Meister Eckhart the great mystic of the Middle Ages spoke of "the little spark" that enlightens the soul. On eight different occasions the Course also refers to "the little spark" which can enlighten the mind. Transcendentalist philosopher Henry David Thoreau like Socrates also spoke of one's "inner genius." Even in contemporary mythologies like the original Star Wars series the Holy Spirit may be thought of as "The Force."

Jesus' 40-days and 40-night experience, alone in the desert is crucial to his deepening awareness of the ever in-dwelling presence of God. There is not one single word of ministry until after Jesus' desert experience. And then we read: *After that he began to preach saying, "The Kingdom of Heaven is at hand."* Meaning, the Kingdom of Heaven is immediately available to anyone, at any time.

The Holy Spirit is the Voice for God, "the Communication Link between God and ourselves; the mechanism of miracles; the highest communication medium; the memory of God we brought with us into this dream; the one who sees our illusions and leads us through them to the Truth (Knowledge). The Holy Spirit is *the non-ego presence in our minds.* A favorite definitions of the Holy Spirit and of God is the *Presence of Holiness* which lives in everything that lives. And so, he lives in your mind, and in the mind of everyone, indeed, in everything that lives. Do we recognize this ever-present presence, or are we distracted by "the world"?

The ego is simply an illusory voice that says it is real. It is the king, "the" authority, the ruler of the mind, and so, it tries to push Spirit out. It is easy to know when we are in ego. The ego is that which judges, interprets, rejects, evaluates, and condemns. It is that which finds fault, criticizes, attacks others and defends itself. The Course is asking us to be aware of this unseen culprit, this virus which would attack God's own invulnerable mind and drive us mad with attack thoughts and judgments we would then throw out upon the world. "Doing the Course," in the first instance is simply being aware of how judgmental we are.

How simple the process is really, to let the Holy Spirit be, *what he is, and seek not to make of love an enemy.* And then, in the same way to let others be who they are. The more we put the ego aside, the greater our awareness that we are not alone, the more we can literally be "inspired," the more we know that God lives within us and goes with us wherever we go.

If you knew Who walks beside you
on the way that you have chosen,
fear would be impossible.
ACIM TEXT-18.III.3:2

Epistle 17

Who Pulls the Puppet's Strings?

The world has not yet experienced
any comprehensive reawakening or rebirth.
Such a rebirth is impossible
as long as you continue to project or miscreate.
It still remains within you, however,
to extend as God extended His Spirit to you.
In reality this is your only choice,
because your free will was given you
for your joy in creating the perfect.
ACIM TEXT-2.I.3:7-10

The Course tells us that "*This is an insane world, and we should not underestimate the extent of its insanity.*" While happiness cannot be found "in" the world. Lesson 287 from the Course asks us to say to ourselves: "*Where would I go but Heaven? What could be a substitute for happiness?*" I can be on vacation, lying on my yacht with a sunny clear blue sky above, and my mind racked in guilt. Or I may be in a prison cell and my mind at rest. It is where the mind is that matters, regardless of where the body may be or what condition it may be in.

Jesus in the Gospel of Luke tells us: "*The Kingdom of Heaven is inside of you.*" It is not in the body. It is in the mind because *the mind belongs* to the spirit which God created and which is therefore eternal. Furthermore, only the mind is real. The ego, on the other hand, sees the body as "the be all" and "the end of all." The body is not the end, and it is not the beginning. It is a temporary figure in our dream and therefore "no thing." The body is at best a tool, which when placed in the hands of Spirit can be a handy learning device, we can use to help find our way Home.

I once had a good friend named Ted, now passed, whom I dearly loved. We were roommates in college, and after college in the summer of '64, we toured Europe on Vespa motor-scooters. Ted was a sweet soul who would later become a disabled Vietnam vet. I stayed at his home once when I was on a lecture tour through Texas. While

51

SUNDAYS WITH MUNDY

there, I could not help but notice his morning routine. After the obligatory trip to the bathroom, he would go to the kitchen, open the refrigerator door, take out a can of beer, flip open the tab on top, sit down at his kitchen table, light a cigarette, and stare at the floor. Question: Who opened that refrigerator door? Who popped the top on the can of beer? Who lit the cigarette? Who issues the directions that anybody follows? Who pulls the puppet's strings?

The body thinks no thoughts.
It has no power to learn, to pardon, nor enslave.
It gives no orders that the mind need serve,
nor sets conditions that it must obey.
ACIM TEXT-31.III.4:2–4

We misuse the body when we "overdo pleasure" and often unconsciously and unwittingly open ourselves to an addiction. We misuse the body when we take pride in its muscles, its beauty; or when we use its brain, lips, tongue, throat, arms, and legs as instruments of attack.

Condemnation never works. Someone asked me what I thought of a well-known personality who is daily in the news. I said that I did not "think" about this individual, meaning I had no words of judgment, of either praise or condemnation, which I would like to share. Sharing always "amplifies." What would you like to amplify?

God's plan is simple;
never circular and never self-defeating.
He has no Thoughts except the Self-extending,
and in this your will must be included.
ACIM TEXT-21.V.6:1-2

To self-extend simply means to love the world regardless of what the world seems to throw our way. Knowing Heaven means being awake and alive even in an insane world.

God wills perfect happiness
for all who will accept their Father's gifts as theirs.
ACIM WORKBOOK-101

Epistle 18

Time, Revelation and Miracles

There is a story about a rabbi who is teaching a group of students. One student puts forth a theory, to which the rabbi responds, "You're right." Another student then puts forth another proposition antithetical to the first student, to which the rabbi says, "You're right." To which a third student observes that seeing how the two students put forward opposite positions they cannot both be right, to which the rabbi says, "You're right!"

The distinction between the past, present and future
is only a stubbornly persistent illusion.
— Albert Einstein

How can we reconcile these two seemingly opposing positions? The answer is that both are true in time. But only one is true in eternity, and eternity is all that there is. In a similar way we could say that reincarnation is true in time, but not in eternity. Why go from dream (life), to dream (life), to dream (life)? Would it not be better to wake up and get off the merry-go-round?

The miracle is a learning device that lessens the need for time.
It establishes an out-of-pattern time interval not under
the usual laws of time. In this sense it is timeless.
ACIM TEXT Principle 47 of the 50 Miracle Principles

There are certain "laws of time." For example, we learn in time; likewise, everything decays in time, i.e., grows older. Heaven, on the other hand, is a changeless state. It is hard to understand changelessness or timelessness outside the realm of eternity. In fact, the Course suggests we not try to figure it out within the context of time. What is needed then is the mystic's point of view, or the inner knowing or revelation.

"Are dreams real?" They seem to be at the time the dream is being experienced. Dreams take place in time. We seem to be "going someplace." We are on an adventure. In dreams, different events keep happening before us "in time." *A Course in Miracles* tells us that this world is a dream, a temporal classroom. *A Course of Love* says that this world is a school. The *miracle, time* and the body are all

53

"learning devices," which are to be transcended once their usefulness is over. If time, like the body, has a beginning and an end, how can something that is not eternal be real?

"There comes a time when the mind takes a higher plane of knowledge but can never prove how it got there."
— Albert Einstein

Enter Revelation

The answer comes in revelation, which also stands outside of time. Revelation can induce an experience so intensely personal it cannot be meaningfully translated into words. Words after all, be they written, spoken or even thought, are "forms," and revelation transcends the form of words. It is impossible to describe an experience of inner knowing. Revelation is literally unspeakable because it is an experience of unspeakable love.

Do the practice, study the Course, and then step out of the way. *A Course of Love* tells us to let our heart guide our way—trust it and we will know what to do in a wordless way.

Epistle 19

The Course as a Deterrent for Alzheimer's

"A cheerful heart is good medicine."
Proverbs 17:22

We have known for a long time that physical exercises, including 'fun things' like simply walking, swimming, dancing, and tennis, are important deterrents in the development of dementia and Alzheimer's. More recently, I came across a study done by Dr. Natalie Marchant, from the University College London, which concluded that depression and anxiety are known factors for dementia. Another study showed that cognitive activity: reading, writing, doing crossword puzzles, studying music, math, or other languages, and engaging in scientific research, also reduces the likelihood of dementia and Alzheimer's.

The Course is not a religion. It is not based on rites and rituals, the repetition of creeds, or the need to follow a list of prescribed rules. The Course is a study that helps us to expose the false beliefs we hold about ourselves and others – thus facilitating the process by which we can forgive both ourselves as well as our brothers and sisters – for what they did not do. What is required is a change of mind, which frees us from depression, anxiety, and our own insanity.

The Course can thus be a deterrent to Alzheimer's since in both reading the Course and in doing the exercises in the Workbook, one is steadily coaxed into thinking more deeply and more lovingly. It, therefore, helps us to find freedom from superficial thinking, leading us to both greater physical and mental health.

The Course is built on a deep and solid foundation, i.e., on the teachings of Jesus, on depth psychology, and on the insights of physics and a meaningful understanding of space/time and the mind. It is not surprising that the Course was given to two deep thinkers and Professors of Psychology at Columbia University. Helen and Bill were influenced by Freud and Jung and their research on the nature of the unconscious and how the unconscious ego determines our attitudes and outlook on life.

The Course may then be thought of as an 'attitude adjustment' to a more positive state of mind, as we give up our attack thoughts, our attachment to the world, and temporal worldly pleasures in exchange for a more peaceful state of mind. Thereby, we learn to let others be who they are, so we can more clearly be who 'we' already are – blessed children of an all-wise mother-father God.

The Course is a study, of the nature of the psyche of humankind. It provides us with exercises we can do that will free us from often-overburdening guilt and depression, thus opening our minds to a clearer way of 'seeing' and 'being' in the world. Indeed, the more deeply we dig into the Course, the more likely we are to come to repeated 'ah ha's and revelatory experiences.

Incantations, repeating creeds, engaging in rites and rituals, and/or ardently following a list of rules does not open the door to Heaven. That is a form of magic. Miracles, on the other hand, are natural signs of forgiveness. Through miracles, we accept God's forgiveness by extending it to others. Miracles represent a change of mind about the world – not a change 'of' the world. If the mind does not change – nothing changes. Understanding how our attitudes, how "projection makes perception," and how we can forgive and let go changes everything.

In January of 2022, I spent some time with Diederik Wolsak at his retreat center in Costa Rica. He does not just teach the Course; he has a way of digging down, finding the uncomfortable scars we all have in our psyche, and exposing them in such a way that "through forgiveness" they can be healed. The result again is freedom from depression and anxiety and a clearer, more centered, mind – along with a greater feeling of love for our neighbor, indeed for the whole of life.

There is a saying, "We become what we study," or "We become what we think about." The Course is therefore simply a process by which we can change our mind about our minds – which moves us from sickness to health, from the limitations of space, time, and a body to eternity.

Studying the Course is a healthful, helpful process and practice. The more we study, the more comfortable and automatic the process of opening to the truth, and thus to love, becomes.

Take it deeper and you will see
that your mind can forever be
bright and clear and eternally free.

Epistle 20

One Brother Is All Brothers

One brother is all brothers.
Every mind contains all minds,
for every mind is one. Such is the truth.
A Course in Miracles W-161.4:1-3

Does Difference Make a Difference?
What is the difference between an enlightened
person and an unenlightened person?
Answer:
The unenlightened person sees a difference.

According to Principle Number 40 of the 50 Miracle Principles of the Course, "*The miracle acknowledges everyone as your brother and mine. It is a way of perceiving the universal mark of God.*" All non-dual teachings affirm that God is One. For example, the *Zohar,* the masterwork of the Kabbalah from the Jewish tradition, tells us that despite appearances—like the waves in the ocean, the sparkle of a single sunbeam, or the sound of one note on a flute in an orchestra—all things *are interdependently* part of one magnificent whole.

God is not in you in a literal sense; you are part of Him.
ACIM TEXT-5.II.5:5

The opening paragraph of the Course tells us that "*The opposite of love is fear but what is all-encompassing can have no opposite.*" Fear has no place in Heaven or in our hearts. Where Heaven is, only Love and Truth prevail. It *appears as though* there are two kinds of minds—the ego-mind, and a Divine Mind. However, the ego has "no" reality. You sometimes hear it said that one should kill the ego. Yet, how can you "kill" something that does not exist? Killing is cruel. There is nothing to kill, as the ego simply dissolves once we see its non-reality.

There is only one Mind,
just as there is only one Will.

This you are afraid of as you believe this statement threatens your independence, something you consider a state of being to be highly

SUNDAYS WITH MUNDY

prized. This statement, however, more rightly confirms your interdependence and your wholeness.—A Course of Love T-31.1:1-2

In the ego's version of Heaven,
we get to keep our individuality.
KEN WAPNICK

We give energy to the ego, when we find fault with, attack, complain, or condemn that which "seems" different. Especially very different like a different race or religion.

God does not forgive because He has never condemned.
ACIM WORKBOOK-46.1:1

Shankara (eighth century, India) is regarded as the first to provide a broad exposition on non-dualism or *Vedanta*. His works describes the unity of Atman (Self) and Brahman (God). In the same way, when Jesus says, "I and the Father are one," he is simply recognizing who he is in truth.

Your holiness is beyond every restriction of time,
space, distance, and limits of any kind.
ACIM WORKBOOK-38.1:2

The definition of Jesus in The Manual for Teachers of the Course says: "*Jesus was a man who saw the face of Christ in all his brothers and sisters and remembered God. So, he became identified with "Christ", a man no longer, but at one with God.*" How did Jesus become the Christ? *By seeing the face of Christ in all his brothers and sisters.* In like manner, in another instance, in the text Jesus says, "*To see me is to see me in everyone.*" What is it that sees?

There are not two things: one, the screen and two,
the document or image. There is just the screen.
Contemporary Non-dual teacher Rupert Spira

What do you "see" when you look upon the world—is it a fearful place? Are other people wrong? Do "they" need to be fixed? What is doing the seeing? *God sees no contradictions* –ACIM WORKBOOK-193.2:1 *And there is no condemnation in God.* –ACIM TEXT-11.IV.8:2

*The body is a limit
imposed on the universal communication
that is an eternal property of mind.
But the communication is internal.*
ACIM TEXT-18.VI.8:3-4

Universal communication is always open to everyone. It comes by way of "revelation." As we get out of our own way, the eyes, the ears, and the mind opens; the flow begins within. And the more we know, the more we know that we know! This is not arrogance. Quite the contrary—with deep inner knowing, there comes a quiet peaceful heart.

We are now experiencing an expansion in consciousness. Slowly, slowly, bit by bit—but also growing exponentially—all seeming differences are being brought into awareness where they can be melted away by the gentle warmth of the Son. We are awakening to the knowledge that *one brother is all brothers; one sister is all sisters.* Hold on and enjoy the ride. Only God is real and there is nothing to be afraid of. As lessons are learned and coexistence affirmed, we remember who we always have been.

Say with me:
*Only my condemnation injures me.
Only my forgiveness sets me free.*
ACIM WORKBOOK-198.9:3-4

Epistle 21

Knowing Our Father's Will

There is no question but one
you should ever ask of yourself.
"Do I want to know my Father's Will for me?"
ACIM TEXT-8.VI.8:1

The thought of God as an all wise and loving father can be found in all the world's religious traditions. God may also be thought of as mother. As the nineteenth century English novelist William Makepeace Thackery said. *"Mother is the name for God on the hearts and minds of children."* I was watching our three-year old grand-daughter Avery Rose when she tripped and fell. She instantly began to cry, calling out! *"I want mommy!"* When it was her grand-father who came to her rescue—she was content.

Oneness is simply the idea God is.
And in His Being, He encompasses all things.
No mind holds anything but Him.
We say, "God is," and then we cease to speak,
for in that knowledge words are meaningless.
There are no lips to speak them,
and no part of mind sufficiently distinct to feel
that it is now aware of something not itself.
It has united with its Source.
And like its Source Itself, it merely is.
ACIM WORKBOOK-169.5:1-9

Putting all division aside we are left with 'God Is and I am'. Call God what you will, Allah, Wano Tango, Jehovah, Yahweh. It matters not the name. "I and the Father are one." Because he is of one mind—so must we be.

All miracles mean life, and God is the Giver of life.
His Voice will direct you very specifically.
You will be told all you need to know.
ACIM TEXT Principle 4 from the 50 Miracles Principles

The words "father" or "mother" represents our relationship with that which gives us Life. God is the Creator, the Source of all Being

Knowing Our Father's Will

and all Life. God's fatherhood or motherhood is established by our existence. God is Cause. We are the Effect. As God is omniscient:

God knows His children with perfect certainty.
He created them by knowing them.
He recognizes them perfectly.
When they do not recognize each other,
they do not recognize Him.
ACIM TEXT-3.III.7:9-12

God has not only created us; he created us perfect. Only in some nightmare-dream could we live standing outside of God's Will and His Eternal Love. We know of that Love as we follow his Will. The 4th and 5th sentences in the Course tell us that: *Free will does not mean that you can establish the curriculum. It means only that you can elect what you want to take at a given time.*

How long, will we wait, how long must we be recalcitrant children? How long will we put off the inevitable reward of knowing God and his Kingdom? I was talking with a man who had been caught in an addiction for twenty years. Finally, finally, he literally fell to his knees and cried out for help and the Course came into his life. He began to read, to do the lessons and a miracle occurred. He did not need a lot of will power. He simply stopped the drinking. How long can we resist our own will, which is God's Will?

All real pleasure comes from doing God's Will.
This is because "not" doing it is a denial of Self.
ACIM TEXT-1.VII.1:4-5

A Course in Miracles may be thought of as a very clear "guide-book," in helping us find our way home leading us to a place where we too in all humility may also say, "I and the Father are one." This is not arrogance. It is an acceptance of our Reality.

And yet, unless your will is one with His,
His gifts are not received.
The power of decision is my own.
This day I will accept myself
as what my Father's Will created me to be.
ACIM WORKBOOK-152.11:3

SUNDAYS WITH MUNDY

I need but keep in mind my Father's Will
for me is only happiness,
to find that only happiness has come to me.
ACIM WORKBOOK-235.1:2

Happiness is inevitable when the Kingdom of God is in sight.

Epistle 22

Wake Up - Get Up - Clean Up
Grow Up - Show Up

This is a course in mind training.
All learning involves attention and study at some level.
ACIM TEXT-1.VI.4:1

Wake Up! *A Course in Miracles* is not the only spirituality that says our life in this world is a dream. The Armenian philosopher and mystic G.I. Gurdjieff (1866-1949) said that almost everyone was "sleep walking" every day, all through the day. We can only awaken, said Gurdjieff, in so far as we recognize that "we have been sleeping." The ego, says the Course, seeks to keep our will (self-awareness) asleep. We thus knock ourselves out with an over-abundance of food, drugs, alcohol, television and, more than anything, the prejudicial points of view that make up our dream world. Daydreams tell us that the problems we see are not of our own making. Someone else is irresponsible! The Course then calls upon us to shake off the ego's stupor and be fully awake and alive participants in life. As Jordan Peterson, author of *The Twelve Rules for Life*, says: "Accept the terrible responsibility of life with eyes wide open."

Look straight at every image that rises to delay you.
The goal is inevitable because it is eternal.
ACIM TEXT-12.II.5:6

Get Up—feet on the floor, shoulders back, stand-up straight. We are called upon to face life directly no matter what life throws our way. Be honest, be clear, do what you are being asked to do. Pay attention. Let's not say that we do not know what to do. Life has meaning and purpose; and if we think that's not true, just dig a little deeper, and that purpose will become increasingly clear.

Miracles are everyone's right,
but purification is necessary first.
ACIM TEXT Principle No. 7 of the 50 Miracle Principles

Clean Up—your body, your finances, surroundings, and relationships. What can you do to have a healthier body, perhaps lose some weight? Feeling depressed and you don't know what to do—start cleaning. There is something about putting the world around us in order that begins to bring life into order. Admiral William McRaven's book *Make Your Bed* reinforces the fact that little things matter. If we can't do little things right, it's harder to do big things right.

Why should you condone insane thinking?
You may believe that you are responsible for what you do,
but not for what you think.
The truth is that you are responsible for what you think.
ACIM TEXT-2.VI.2:3&5

Grow Up—do the work, learn the lesson, forgive everyone. The number of enemies we should have in life is zero. When I hear politicians talk about China, Russia, or Iran as our enemies there is something amiss. We are all just people here. Can we not transcend the idea of enemies? When, in Matthew 10:36, Jesus says: "A man's enemies are those of his own house," he does not mean our brothers and sisters. He means the enemy inside our own heads (thoughts). Our main forgiveness task comes in forgiving ourselves. There is no ego. There is no enemy. Look with love upon the world at all times and in all places.

Look out from the perception of your own holiness
to the holiness of others.
ACIM TEXT-1.III.6:7

Show Up—There are plenty of folks who need assistance. Let's do what we can to help, even in a small way. I have a neighbor who goes on daily walks. He takes along a small plastic bag, like something you would get from a grocery or drug store, and when he sees some trash along the way, he puts it in the bag, brings it home and throws it away. It's a small thing, but it helps to keep our neighborhood clean.

Epistle 23

Maintaining Sanity in an Insane World

*I have often said that a person who wishes to begin a good life
should be like a circle. Let him get the center in the right place
and keep it so and the circumference will be Good.*
MEISTER ECKHART
German priest and mystic (1260-1326)

*This is an insane world,
and do not underestimate the extent of its insanity.
There is no area of your perception that it has
not touched, and your dream is sacred to you.
That is why God placed the Holy Spirit in you,
where you placed the dream.*
ACIM TEXT-14.I.2:6-8

This is an insane world insofar as it is the ego's world. The ego has always fought for dominance, and it is likely to stay that way for some time. Although the ego rules the world, the ego does not have to rule your mind. This is "a course" in Mind training, and we are given two simple choices either "we can let" the ego-mind rule, or we can let "The Voice for God," the Holy Spirit be our guide. We are each in charge of our own decision making.

*I have a kingdom I must rule...
I thus direct my mind, which I alone can rule.
And thus, I set it free to do the Will of God.*
W-236.1:1,7-8

A study of history is a study of wars. A study of the Course is a study in that which makes peace. A few years ago, Dolores and I were invited to Japan where I gave several lectures. After an all-day Saturday seminar, a group of us went to a nice restaurant. At some point the conversation turned to World War II, and I asked our host "Why did Japan decide to attack the United States?" He replied, "Because, in arrogance, we thought we could win."

The Authority Problem

The ego in search of an earthly kingdom is not only not loving, but it can also be quite insensitive and hurtful. Egos go to war. Spirit stays home looking to enrich the life within. Rather than getting caught in projection, the Course asks us to turn within, to study the daily lessons, listen to the Voice for God, undo our own errors, and responsibly correct them. It is not our job to try and fix our neighbor. Rather are we to "love our neighbor as ourselves." The Atonement is a process by which we learn to let go of any need to assert ourselves over our brothers and sisters. We are to seek for surcease and rest from the projective, judgmental mind. Projecting makes us weak— extending love makes us strong.

Being within the presence of God means finding peace and tranquility within, despite the insanity which whirls about within this world. The ego is on the outlook for trouble. There is a cartoon of a waiter who goes up to a table where folks are obviously engaged in gossip and says, "Good afternoon, folks, is *anything* all right?"

I like French Philosopher Voltaire's (1694-1778) saying,
Opinions have caused more trouble on this little earth
than plagues or earthquakes.
and
German Scientist, George Lichtenberg's (1742-1799) saying,
Nothing is more conducive to peace of mind
than not having an opinion.

Can you watch the news, without letting it take the peace of God away from you? According to the Course, the ego perpetually throws us off balance by raising control, rather than sanity, to predominance.

Remember
There is a place in you where
this whole world has been forgotten,
where no memory of sin and of illusion lingers still.
There is a place in you which time has left,
and echoes of eternity are heard.
ACIM TEXT-29.V.1:1-5

Epistle 24

The Classroom Called Life

Sometimes life takes on a surrealistic feel. It was that way on 9/11; with Covid, political upheaval, and social unrest. Sometimes life feels a bit like a science fiction movie. Yet beyond every dream, there stands an awakening and a greater awareness. We see this change in the demise of the church and in an awakening that is happening on Zoom, in podcasts, on YouTube, and in the growth of consciousness expanding programs on new media like *Gaia* and *Conscious Vitality*. There is a whole host of teachers out there, offering deeper and more profound ways of seeing and being.

The deeper we dive into this sea of universal consciousness the more meaningful life becomes. The changes we are experiencing now can, and will, help us awaken—if we are willing to let them change us. Clearly, this is no time to go back to sleep. Indeed, we are being called upon to accept responsibility at yet deeper levels.

From the most ancient of mystical traditions, we hear the story of a young man or woman who goes off alone or perhaps together on a journey of discovery. They are headed to Mecca or maybe, as with Henry David Thoreau, to a cabin on a small lake called Walden Pond. We all are looking to learn 'something.' There is an awakening going on, and now, it is ever more intense, because this time, thanks to technology, the whole world is involved.

Simply put, this world is in no way ultimate reality. Rather is it a school for souls; and we have been given certain "learning devices" to work with that include a body, a mind, time, and an inner guide. The body is a vehicle, a computer, and a communication device. Like all learning devices, the body is temporal. It is here for us to use until its usefulness is over. We are the mind, i.e., the driver; the body is the machine, and it is essential to keep our vehicles in good working order. The roads we choose to go down determine the lessons we learn along the way. It behooves us to learn our lessons now, lest we be held back and asked to repeat a grade or two. We have been given a *Textbook,* a *Workbook,* and a *Teachers Manual,* along with a vast array of other writings, both ancient and modern, filled with inspiration and insights from other student/teachers. Our primary text has been written by a perfect teacher who, in time, completed the atonement long ago. We have not been left comfortless. Jesus tells us:

As a man and also one of God's creations,
my right thinking, which came from the Holy Spirit
or the Universal Inspiration,
taught me first and foremost that this Inspiration is for all.
ACIM TEXT-5.I.4:6

This eternal-internal teacher we call "the Holy Spirit" is with us, always, to help us see what Jesus saw. The time in which we take our lessons is voluntary. It is up to us to decide whether we will choose to listen to this wise guide. There are many other students in this school, and it is incumbent upon us to work together so that we might graduate together.

One of our lessons comes in the recognition of our inherent equality, regardless of our vehicle's outward form. It is, after all, the soul, not the body, that resides in Heaven. And the soul has nothing to do with sex, age, color of skin, geography, level of education, wealth, looks, or any of a vast array of possible differences, which do not make a difference.

Only while there is a belief in differences
is learning meaningful.
ACIM TEXT-2.II.5:8

Some of the classes we sign up for can be rather difficult. There is a classroom called "marriage," another called "children," another called "divorce," another called "bankruptcy." There is one called "cancer," and in the end, the classroom called "death." With death, if not before, there is the final lesson of the Atonement and Love Universal. Clearly, to graduate, we must undo the ego. Ultimately, we find that those who die do not die when the body dies. We are not what we seem, i.e., we are not the learning device itself, rather are we like Jesus the Christ.

Say with me:
I will there be light.

Epistle 25

Health is Inner Peace

The opposite of joy is depression.
When your learning promotes depression instead of joy,
you cannot be listening to God's joyous Teacher
and learning His lessons.
ACIM TEXT-8.VII.13:1-2

Depression arises when we choose to follow the promptings of the ego rather than listening to our inner guide. When we are depressed, we are not at peace because someplace deep inside "we know" we are not fulfilling the function God has given us. When we choose selfishness over selflessness or anger over serenity, we cannot but feel guilty, even though we may bury that guilt so deep we are unaware of the cause of our distress.

The continuing decision to remain separated
is the only possible reason for continuing guilt feelings.
ACIM TEXT-5.V.8.1:

"I Can't Believe I Ate the Whole Thing"

The ego has three primary uses for the body: namely, for attack, for pleasure, and for pride. We feel guilty when we attack, when we overdo pleasure, and when we judge ourselves as better than or inferior to our brothers and sisters. Let's take one example: if we over-pleasure the body, rather than practicing moderation, we are disappointed in ourselves for our lack of self-control and discipline.

There was an Alka-Seltzer ad in the early 70's that shows a big fellow sitting on the side of his bed in his pajamas, and he keeps saying: "*I can't believe I ate the whole thing.*" "*I can't believe I ate the whole thing.*" He had been gluttonous, and now, he is paying the price for his excessiveness; and of course, the fix for his predicament is Alka-Seltzer. But Alka-Seltzer is only a temporary-physical fix. What we really need to do is to make choices from our right-mind, instead of repeatedly following the ego's guidance.

Reason will tell you that the only way to escape from misery
is to recognize it and go the other way.
ACIM TEXT-22.II.4:1

Choose Once Again

Who runs this mind of mine? Who decides to attack (in thought, word or deed)? Who decides to over-pleasure the body? Who chooses to be arrogant and filled with pride? "Choose Once Again" is the title of the last section in the last chapter of the Course. Jesus wants to reassure us that we can make a choice which will bring us joy, instead of pain.

The Course asks us to be vigilant and watchful. Getting angry, getting caught in an addiction, being thoughtless and boastful, all these things are fixable. The "fix" is the miracle—a miracle being simply a correction in perception. We may go "off course," but we can always bring the mind back in line with The Mind of God. And when we do, depression goes, and joy comes to fill the space depression once occupied. How often we hear of the joy of someone who has truly let an addiction go. It is like Heaven to them, as they now see another world the ego's eyes could never find.

There is a very simply solution—choose once again.

It is your thoughts alone that cause you pain.
Nothing external to your mind
can hurt or injure you in any way.
There is no cause beyond yourself
that can reach down and bring oppression.
No one but yourself affects you.
There is nothing in the world that has the power
to make you ill or sad, or weak or frail.
ACIM WORKBOOK-190.5:1-5

Say with me:
"I choose the joy of God instead of pain."

Epistle 26

Escaping Forever Our Self-Made Cell

Nothing made by a child of God is without power.
It is essential to realize this, because otherwise
you will be unable to escape from the prison you have made.
ACIM TEXT-3.VII.1:7-8

A man is climbing alone in the mountains. He comes to the edge of a precipice, looks over the side, develops vertigo, loses his balance, and falls. Quickly, he reaches out and grabs hold of the branch of a small tree. Suspended hundreds of feet in the air, unable to think of anything else, he cries out: "Is anybody there?" There is a long silence, and then a voice from out of nowhere says: "It's all right, my son, I'm here. I will take care of you. Let go." There is another long silence, and the man says: "Is anybody else there?"

There are no miracles in Heaven. Only in an illusory world are miracles needed to dispel fear and bring peace to our divided minds. Lesson 101 from the Course says that "*God's Will for Me is Perfect Happiness.*" Really, "Perfect Happiness?"

In 2016 I wrote a book titled Lesson 101: *Perfect Happiness.* Almost everyone who read it gave it a five-star review, and yet it did not sell well I think, in part, because of the title. No one believes in "perfect" happiness. According to the Course, this world is dominated by our divided minds. Consequently, we get to have a little happiness "sometimes," sprinkled in along with a good bit of ambiguity, angst, and attack thoughts.

As it is, we invent the world we see. And we hang out in our self-made cells, begging for release, all the while the door was never locked. Or, as the Course says most clearly, we each make up the prison in which we see ourselves (W-57.2:2). The lessons we give ourselves seem hard indeed. And, yet, who is it that builds with every bitter brick, day by day, the cell we see?

Condemn and you are made a prisoner.
Forgive and you are free.
ACIM WORKBOOK-198.2:103

In fault-finding and condemnation of our brothers and sisters, we inevitably feel guilty— although that guilt is often buried so deeply, we do not see the cause of our suffering as all self-made. I knew a man who got fired from his job because of his anger. And then, with no helpful job reference, he could not find work. And then he could not pay his mortgage; and then he had no home and was put out on the street. Yet, to hear him tell it—it was all someone else's fault. We attack the world and then wonder why the world is so dark, and love is missing. There really is a simple answer. As the Course expresses it: "To have, give all to all." Meanwhile, the ego is saying, "No, it's to have, take all from all."

Like an alcoholic, we cling to our bottle of despair, begging God not to take it from us. And yet it is only as we choose our own release that we can be set free. God cannot make our decisions for us. Only "we" can set ourselves free. And then we find that following the Voice for God is the most blessed experience. A simple decision is required and nothing more. All we have to do is accept responsibility for the cell in which we think we live, and then forgive ourselves— for being the one who made our lives so miserable. It is we who free ourselves from our self-imposed prison. It is really a simple decision. Love "everything" and condemn nothing.

Say with me:
"I will forgive, and this will disappear."

Epistle 27

Love Longing for Itself

"Underneath it all, we really love each other."
Love can easily get covered over with ego emissions and all the
judgments we so easily throw out upon the world.
Thus, it is that...

Projection will always hurt you.
It reinforces your belief in your own split mind,
and its only purpose is to keep the separation going.
It is solely a device of the ego to make you feel
different from your brothers and separated from them.
Projection and attack are inevitably related,
because projection is always a means of justifying attack.
Anger without projection is impossible.
The ego uses projection only to destroy your perception
of both yourself and your brothers.
ACIM TEXT-6.II.3:1-3,5-7

I knew a man whose father was rough, difficult, and demanding. The son had a lot of trouble dealing with his father and often felt as though he hated him. Then one day the father, who was getting older, was hit by a car while crossing the street in New York City. He broke his hip, some blood clots formed, and then, he suffered a stroke. He never fully recovered. After that, he became childlike, innocent—and loving. The love was in him all along --- longing for expression.

Now the man whom the son hated was altogether different and he was dependent upon his son to care for him. What a dilemma! The old man, whom the son had hated, was no longer hateful. Now, he was uncomplicated, trusting. He smiled frequently and looked to his son for support. As the son was willing to let go of the past, a healing occurred. All that was left, all that was real between them, was love. Life is like that: buried within, sometimes not even too deeply, love is trying to find a way out, and an opportunity for expression. Thus, our only job is one of "removing the blocks to an awareness of loves presence."

Unforgiveness means holding onto something we reinforce in our minds and make real because we do not want to look at ourselves and how it is that we have contributed to what we see as someone else's problem. If someone attacks you, for any reason—remember they are hurting. And because they are hurting—the healing can come only by our extending the gentle balm of love. Once, when I was working with someone who was suffering from a deep depression, I asked Jesus how was I supposed to help this person? And I heard: "Just keep loving him." What a simple answer—and it is true—it is how miracles work.

Miracles are natural.
When they do not occur, something has gone wrong.
ACIM TEXT Principle 6 of the 50 Miracle Principles says,

Everything that comes from love is natural. The ego is not natural. When we're in ego we feel uneasy, uncomfortable. Something is missing. Relaxing into love, it is possible to love everything—all those around you, your pets and every experience that comes your way.

Love always leads to love.
The sick, who ask for love, are grateful for it,
and in their joy they shine with holy thanks.
ACIM TEXT-13.VI.10:4

Epistle 28

Above The Battleground

There is no safety in a battleground.
You can look down on it in safety
from above and not be touched.
But from within it you can find no safety.
ACIM TEXT-23.III.6:5-7

Sometimes, when I am giving a presentation on the Course and I'm asked for a "take away"—something one might use as a guide from the Course—I will say: "*Yes, very simply, remember: Do not attack!* Attack is always, always a mistake." Egos do not respond well to attack and are most likely to become defensive and attack back. Furthermore,

If you attack error in another, you will hurt yourself.
You cannot know your brother when you attack him.
Attack is always made upon a stranger.
You are making him a stranger by misperceiving him,
and so you cannot know him.
ACIM TEXT-3.III.7:1-4

I would not want to be involved in politics because being involved in politics often means seeking out sin in a brother or sister, as though pointing out our neighbor's faults makes us better. There is a corollary to "Do not attack"; namely, "Do not defend." Lesson No. 153 from the Workbook of the Course states: "*In defenselessness my safety lies.*" If someone attacks your body, you will naturally do whatever you can to protect your body. However, we are not talking here about defending the body; we are talking about defending the ego-oriented mind.

Defenselessness is all that is required for the truth
to dawn upon our minds with certainty.
ACIM WORKBOOK-135.21:3

While defenses seem to protect us from our guilt, fear, and attack by others, they make us more insecure and afraid. Ultimately, we stand naked before God. There is no effective attack, blame, or defense to be offered before God against any person. Excuses do not work in Heaven, and they do not work here.

Handling Criticism

What should we do when someone has a criticism of us? Listen! Listen very carefully and ask:

1. Why is this person saying what he or she is saying?
2. Is there even a grain of truth in what is being said?
3. Is there some way I can make things better?
4. Is there any possibility that I can see this differently?

Maybe those who criticize are right. Maybe they are wrong. If they are wrong, they need my love. If they are right, they need my love. If we are angry and volatile, we must think that there is a reason to be reactive. Being reactive means we need a better way of seeing. For this reason, we need not take too much delight in praise nor be too disheartened with blame.

This person who is critical may be telling me something that no one else will. By listening carefully, I come to understand the other person's point of view, and I come closer to a solution. Listening to the criticism will probably be appreciated. This is "the real meaning" of doing unto others as we would have them do unto us. The only thing that needs correction is the mind's defensiveness.

I watched a bang, bang, shoot 'em up,' get in the cars, and chase each other scene on television. All the good guys or the bad guys had to do to get a fight started was to say something about the other guy's mother. Do we not know the truth of our mother's nature? How silly and impetuous the ego can be to get upset by an obvious falsehood. If something is said against us falsely, this does not mean that we should not say what is true. But to respond in anger is always a mistake.

All anger is an attempt to make someone else feel guilty.
ACIM TEXT-15.VII.10:3

If I am about to attack anyone for any reason, I should ask, "Is this something I would accuse myself of doing?" Not attacking does not mean that we never disagree. It takes skill to be a parent, schoolteacher, counselor, or employer who can deal with difficult situations without anger, attack, or malice.

Good teachers never terrorize their students.
ACIM TEXT-3.I.4:5

Ken Wapnick writes in *A Course in Miracles and Christianity*:

"I have frequently made the comment that one of the most important lessons a Teacher of God can learn is how to disagree with someone without it being an attack." Anger keeps the ego alive, but anger dissipates when we see we have no need for it.

Say with me:
Let every voice but God's be still in me.

Epistle 29

Awakening from the Dreaming

All that we see or seem
Is but a dream within a dream.
Edgar Allen Poe (1809-1849)

You are the dreamer of the world of dreams.
No other cause it has, nor ever will.
ACIM TEXT-27.VII.13:1

The conception of the world as an illusion is as ancient as the Vedas, the world's oldest scriptures. Very simply put, the Vedas tell us: "things are not what they seem." The illusory nature of the world, says the Vedas, takes multitudinous forms in which we see good and bad, love and fear, truth and illusion.

Double Vision

Real seeing, says the Course, "comes not from double vision." Double vision is what happens when we try to look at the world through both the eyes of the ego and the eyes of Spirit. Double vision is not a balanced way of being, since we simply cannot serve both God and mammon (i.e., the ego). Only God, Love, Truth, Eternity is real. The rest is all a fantasy of our own making.

Early on in her scribing of the Course, Jesus told Helen that the Course was coming to us now because the usual slow evolutionary process of spiritual awakening was experiencing a "celestial speedup." That speedup is exponential. The more the speedup grows, the faster it goes. The whole world is going deeper and changing, so let's hold on, remain centered in God, and we will make it through.

There is no world!
This is the central thought
the course attempts to teach.
Not everyone is ready to accept it,
and each one must go as far as he can
let himself be led along the road to truth.

He will return and go still farther,
or perhaps step back a while and then return again.
ACIM WORKBOOK-pI.132.6:3-5

After his enlightenment, the Buddha met a man on the road who was struck by the Buddha's great radiance and his peaceful presence. The man asked, "My friend, what are you? Are you a god?" "No," said the Buddha. "Well, then are you a wizard?" Again, the Buddha answered, "No." So, the man asked, "Are you a man?" "No," said the Buddha. "Well, my friend, then what are you?" And the Buddha replied, "I am awake." In like manner, the Course is all about awakening and remembering who we are in truth.

We are now, out of necessity, experiencing a deeper, more metaphysical level of understanding of the nature of reality as what we call reality comes undone. Remember, the atonement is the undoing of the ego, and the ego does not want to be undone. How do we awaken from the dreaming of the world?

This is a Course on accepting responsibility
for what we think, what we feel, and who we are.
KEN WAPNICK

A clear first step in awakening is the acceptance of responsibility for our personal and collective dreaming. All dreams are projections of the dreamer, be they individual dreams or collective dreams. Collective dreaming the Course calls "the dreaming of the world." We are called upon to accept responsibility for our own projections, our individual dreams. We are called upon to let things be what they are. Our basic responsibility is to clean up our own dream and free ourselves from nightmares.

Stay Out of the Sandbox

It is a good idea not to get caught up in dreaming of the world. The news, the fray, the ranting and raving about who is right and who is wrong can easily pull us off track. One of Ken Wapnick's most consistent pieces of advice when someone told him of their personal drama, tragedy or soap opera was to say: "Stay out of the sandbox." In other words, do not get caught in the dream. Being caught in the dream of the world keeps us from seeing and Being in the Kingdom of Heaven—right here—right now.

Corrective learning always begins with the awakening of spirit,
and the turning away from the belief in physical sight.
ACIM TEXT-2.V.7:1

We are easily distracted by the outside: by our bodies and the things of the world, other people and their behavior, and whatever there is on television. While the body will one day perish, Spirit endures forever. Said in another way, love is the most essential thing in the world; and the ego being, self-centered, knows it not.

Thus, the little Prince
in Antoine de Saint-Exupéry's *Le Petit Prince* says:
And now here is my secret, a very simple secret:
It is only with the heart that one can see rightly;
what is essential is invisible to the eye.

When your body and your ego and your dreams are gone,
you will know that you will last forever.
ACIM TEXT-6.V.A.1:1

Epistle 30

Thinking Miraculously

The world as a state of being,
as a whole, has entered a time,
brought on largely by A Course in Miracles,
in which readiness for miracle-mindedness is upon it.
A COURSE OF LOVE - C:P.5

A Course in Miracles and *A Course of Love* give us newer, deeper ways of seeing and being—if only we can do what they "suggest." We have free will. It is up to us to decide. Shall we continue to follow the wayward ego, or can we turn instead to a very wise guide within?

The power of decision is your last remaining freedom
as a prisoner in this world.
ACIM TEXT-12.VII.9:1

I once asked Ken Wapnick why he thought the Course came to us during the latter quarter of the 20th century. He said he did not know for sure, but he did not believe it could have come to us until after Sigmund Freud, Carl Jung, and the other depth psychologists began telling us about the degree to which the unconscious and the habituated ego are so influential in directing our seeing. Evolution expands exponentially. The faster things progress, the more we grow in breadth and depth of understanding.

Growth in consciousness occurs as older more stalwart, fearful, legalistic, and dogmatic traditions lose some of their grip on an ever-expanding mind. Just over five hundred years ago on January 3, 1521, Martin Luther was excommunicated from the Catholic Church by Pope Leo X. Luther was a deeply religious man. Once he was out and could no longer work within the church, the Protestant Reformation was under way. Before long there would be hundreds of different more open-minded ways of seeing and being. Given time, they too would create their own laws, creeds, dogmas, and rigid system. Five hundred years later, these traditions in turn are in decline.

An expanding consciousness does not stand still. Now, even deeper, clearer, and freer ways of seeing come into view. While there are those who understandably mourn the decline of traditional churches (I loved the singing), a beautiful flower is coming into bloom. Church is no longer a building on the corner. We can now join with those of like-minded consciousness by simply sitting in front of our computer screen and being receptive to Unity and Truth.

Without a rose there is no compost.
Without compost there is no rose.
Tich Nath Hanh (1926-present)

Digging Deeper

When Jesus in Matthew 10:36 says, "A man's foes shall be those of his own household," he was not talking about our brothers and our sisters. One's house is one's head, one's mind. As with any change, we are called upon to look more deeply within. Cartoonist Walt Kelly in 1970, on the occasion of "The First Earth Day," writing about our mistreatment of the planet, had his cartoon character Pogo say: "We have met the enemy and he is us." Once again, "things they are a changing." The ego would have us thinking fearfully, while the Holy Spirit would lead us into a blessed and loving expansion of our awareness.

Trust would settle every problem now.
ACIM TEXT 26.VIII.2:3

Vision, Happiness, and Release from Pain.

Thinking lovingly (i.e., miraculously) leads us into deeper peace and joy. Thinking fearfully leaves us anxious and distressed. Which way do you want to go? The Course asks us to accept responsibility for literally everything that comes our way.

I am responsible for my health, my finances, my relationships, my home, and extended environment. I am responsible for whatever I am thinking and experiencing. It behooves us to make every act count, since we are going to be here for only a short time. Accepting responsibility for being here, in this incredible world at this astonishing moment, we are called upon to be conscientious and to love whatever comes our way. Did you see the movie "The Best Exotic Marigold Hotel"? The last line gives us hope. "Remember, everything works out fine in the end; and if it's not fine, it's not the end."

Epistle 31

I Would Be Happier If. . .

Let us Pull Over, Stop and Look at Where We Are

Every now and then it is a good idea to pull off the road, check our alignment with GPS (God's Plan for Salvation); get quiet for a moment, and look at the view before we proceed. Where am I? Where am I going? Can I give up being such a determined backseat driver and allow God to direct my every turn.

Straight is the way and narrow is the gate
which leads into Life.
Broad is the way and wide is the gate
which leads to destruction and many there are who go there in
MATTHEW 7:13-14

Though the way Home is laid out clearly before us the ego can easily find, diversions, distractions, and trinkets to fill our lives along the way. Many years ago, while traveling and lecturing I stayed with a woman (now deceased) in whose home every room was filled with antiques, so much so that it looked like an antique store. "This is what happens," she said, "when you have a lot of money, and you can't travel."

God's plan is simple.
never circular and never self-defeating.
He has no Thoughts except the Self-extending,
and in this your will must be included.
T-21.V.6:1-2

Self-extending is the ongoing process of creation, wherein Spirit extends itself not in space and time, but rather in an inner expansion of the heart-mind and a growing awareness of God's guiding our lives every second along the way.

Very early on in the Course, in the section immediately following the 50 Miracle Principles there comes a section called "Time, Revelation and Miracles." Jesus wastes no time in getting to the important stuff. Revelation is a way of seeing free of the ego. It represents an 'ah ha.' And when it is deep enough, not just an 'ah ha!' it becomes a rolling Homeric laugh and an 'ah ha, ha, ha, ha!" Many of our problems, says the Course are actually absurd when seen from a sane point of view.

> *Revelation induces only experience.*
> *Miracles, on the other hand, induce action.*
> T-2.II.2:3-4

A little exercise:

You can do this on your computer or find a pen and a piece of paper. Across the top of the page write. "I would be happier if." If what? In short sentences or phrases write down a few things you think would make you happier.

Look over the list.

Be sure to include some things you would like to be free of from literal "things' to negative thoughts and projections. Maybe there is some house cleaning that needs to be done. Maybe we can cut down on some projections by giving politics a rest for a while.

Is there anyone out there you think should be asking you for forgiveness, if so, reverse the process, go to them and ask them to forgive you. This worked well when my daughter was a teenager. Accept others as they are, as you would have yourself accepted. There is a lot of peace of mind to be found in letting. *Let all things be exactly as they are.*

Generalizations do not work i.e. "I'm going to be nicer" does not mean much. Losing weight, the number one New Year's resolution, can be made specific. Put a calendar on the wall above your bathroom scales. Make a note of your weight on the calendar every day at about the same time. If the weight goes up – why? If it goes down why? I find it a simple and effective way to maintain awareness and balance.

The whole purpose of the Course is to help us find Inner Peace. That's it! Is there anything you want more than Inner Peace?

> Say with me:
> *God is in everything I see because God is in my mind.*

Epistle 32

Bringing Order Out of Chaos

In an online class I was teaching on ACIM, I asked the folks: "Why are you here? Why are you attending this class?" Everybody wants an answer to the question "Why are we here?" We literally thirst for an answer, and the Course has an answer. Helen Schucman, the scribe of the Course, once told Jesus that his Course was not working for her. And Jesus responded: *"Why don't you do what I am asking you to do, so you can hear my voice even better?"* Like it or not, we are here. So, how can we live here and be happy? How can we find peace of mind? It is not that there is no answer. The real question is—why don't we do what we feel called to do?

Stop the World I Want to Get Off

Do you remember the musical and movie *Stop the World I Want to Get Off* from the 1960's? The title came from a graffiti and was set with a circus background. It was a story about a fellow named Littlechap who goes off in search of meaning in life. He marries his boss's daughter and has two daughters but wants a son. He allows his growing dissatisfaction with existence to lead him into the arms of various women. (Each of these women is played by the same woman who also plays the role of his wife). Each time something unsatisfactory happens, he calls out: *"Stop the World,"* and Littlechap turns and addresses the audience. Only in old age does he realize that what he really wanted, he already had—the love of his wife and children. In the end, his wife dies, and he must come to terms with his selfishness.

I received a letter from a prisoner who is a subscriber to *Miracle's* magazine. He asked so many questions about the meaning of life that my best answer was to write him a short letter while sending him a copy of ACIM and my book *Living A Course in Miracles*.

All real pleasure comes from doing God's Will.
This is because "not" doing it is a denial of Self.
Denial of Self results in illusions,
while correction of the error brings release from it.

*Do not deceive yourself into believing that you can relate
in peace to God or to your brothers with anything external.*
ACIM TEXT-1.VII.1:4-7

So, What Is God's Will?

We already know the answer to that question, or better, we know
what it is not. It is not our task to bring the Light to the darkness;
our task is to bring the darkness to the Light. As residents of this
world, we know more about the darkness than Light. If we truly
knew the Light, we would Live in the Light. As it is, like Littlechap,
we live in darkness: egotism, greed, and a dozen or more synonyms
thereof, with a little bit of light thrown in.

I was talking with Jeff Seibert, of the Foundation for A Course
in Miracles, which was started by Ken and Gloria Wapnick. He
said they were working on producing a recording of a workshop by
Ken not previously made public titled *Weeding the Garden*. In other
words, cleaning house, or clearing out the garbage, is our first task.
As *we* clean out the garbage (selfishness, lies, greed, etc.), we bring
order into our lives. Another word we could use here would be *sanity*.
An ordered life is a sane life; a sane life is an ordered life. As it is
we give a little bit of attention to the Holy Spirit and a good deal of
attention to the ego.

*The very fact that you can bring any order into chaos
shows you that you are not an ego,
and that more than an ego must be in you.
For the ego "is" chaos, and if it were all of you,
no order at all would be possible.*
ACIM TEXT-14.X.5:5-6

There is something about having the world around us in order
that helps to bring the mind into order. Bringing order can mean
lots of things: engaging in forgiveness, clarifying relationships, being
honest, cleaning up our finances. The Course refers to the body as
a learning device, so it might mean getting this learning device into
better working order. It means practicing forgiveness. It means paying more attention to the guidance of the Holy Spirit—as, ultimately, order is clarified not by us but by the Holy Spirit.

Epistle 33

Stay Safe and Wait:
The Cavalry Is Coming

Tribulation does not make people impatient
*But proves that **they are** impatient.*
Martin Luther

Before I write a Sunday morning epistle, I often sit silently for a moment and ask, "What should I share today?" I like to do this early in the morning while the mind is fresh and rested. It is quiet in the house; the phone is not likely to ring, and my wife Dolores is still sleeping. It is even quiet out front on the street this early in the day. In the distance, I hear a commuter train quickly moving down the tracks taking folks to work in New York City.

The title for this missive came almost immediately to mind: "Stay Safe and Wait" and then I heard, "The Cavalry is Coming." "The cavalry is coming"? Wait-a-minute, the cavalry is an army— armies kill people. And then I remembered hearing that the COVID vaccine is to be distributed by the Department of Health in conjunction with the Department of Defense.

The word 'jihad' has nowhere been
used in the Quran to mean war.
It means "struggle."
The action most consistently called for
in the Quran is the exercise of patience.
Mulana Wahiduddin Khan (1925-2021)

While the Course is clear that ultimately all healing is of the mind. It also tells us that, if any form of fear is present and taking medicine will help to relieve our fear then go ahead and take the medicine. When I had cancer in 2001-2002, I was trying to decide between a natural approach and chemotherapy. I went to see Ken Wapnick and asked his advice. He said, "If you are going to do the natural approach, you have to do it all the way!" Dolores was afraid of my trying a natural approach, and in part to assuage her fears, I took the chemo. I never thought the cancer was going to get me and chemo was a nuisance, I "put up with the nuisance" till the test showed the cancer was all gone.

We are inherently connected to each other through our relationship with God. We cannot help it. It is in our psychic DNA. We find God *through* each other by seeing the other as the Christ—thus reflecting the law of cause and effect which the Course calls "the most fundamental law there is." We become the Christ *by seeing* the Christ in all our brothers and sisters. This is a reversal from the thinking of the suspicious ego that judges "the other" as separate, different from ourselves, and not to be trusted. The ego cannot see equality, thinking of itself as special and therefore often either *better than, or worse than* our neighbor. The ego is never in balance. We have selfishness, even demagoguery, on the one-hand, and/or suffering victimhood on the other.

So, we stay home; we meditate; we read; and we enjoy the benefits of this wonderful new technology called Skype or Zoom, YouTube and/or whatever program we choose. Numerous churches were dying before COVID, and many of the smaller ones may well not survive this pandemic. And yet as churches are dying, a new kind of spiritual community is coming into view—based not on geography, but rather on like-minded seeking of the divine.

In the meantime, we can stay safe, wait, and remember that mastery of the Course comes with consistent patience, application, and study. Patience is one of the ten qualities of a Teacher of God. Indeed, the Course tells us that "Infinite patience produces immediate effects."

> *Those who are certain of the outcome can afford to wait, and wait without anxiety. Patience is natural to the teacher of God. All he sees is certain outcome, at a time perhaps unknown to him as yet, but not in doubt. The time will be as right as is the answer. And this is true for everything that happens now or in the future. The past as well held no mistakes; nothing that did not serve to benefit the world, as well as him to whom it seemed to happen. Patience is natural to those who trust. Sure of the ultimate interpretation of all things in time, no outcome already seen or yet to come can cause them fear.* —A COURSE IN MIRACLES

Say with me from ACIM Workbook Lesson 160
"I am at home. Fear is the stranger here."

Epistle 34

God is Lonely?

Angela Potts Mang'andah, an ACIM leader from Rhode Island sent an email questioning the following sentence from the Course. "*God is lonely without His Sons, and they are lonely without Him.*" Angela asks, "If God is complete how could he be 'missing' something?" This following is an answer to her question.

Dear Angela, as with many things in the Course, this concept of God being lonely is a metaphor. In a similar way, the Course says, "God weeps at the 'sacrifice' of His children who believe they are lost to Him." God who is Love and the whole of the Mind of the Universe does not have tear ducts. If "you" are not in God, then God is "missing" some part of Himself because you are a part of God; and if you, or I, or anyone is not aware of their presence in God, something is amiss.

*God is in everything I see
because God is in my mind.*
ACIM WORKBOOK 30

The ego attempts to think outside of the Mind of God. That "attempt" leads to the making of one's own kingdom external to the Kingdom of Heaven. All the while, there is no kingdom outside of Heaven that has any eternity (reality/truth). What is created by God is timeless, having no beginning or ending. Time and space are one illusion, with many different forms. When our thoughts are projected beyond our minds into the illusory physical world, we perceive our thoughts in terms of time (past and future). The nearer a thought is brought to where we are, or we perceive ourselves as bodies, the more we think of it in terms of the physicality of space/time.

Bodies are time-bound and clearly destructible. Bodies start at a specific minute in time, and they end at a specific minute in time. Spirit is indestructible, having no form. How can you destroy formlessness? The "All in All" cannot be lonely, as we think of loneliness in human terms. You, me, we, are part of God. If any part of the wholeness of God is missing, *"we" are lonely.* We are lonely when we are not at home with God.

The only parable of Jesus mentioned in the Course is the story of the prodigal son. A young man approaches his father and asks for his inheritance, so he can go off on his own. We each inherit a body, and we take off into the world. We are all prodigal sons and daughters. In essence we say: "I would rather do it myself." God does not deny our request. The prodigal son goes into a 'foreign land' and there wastes his inheritance on *riotous living*. Having exhausted his supply, he ends up taking care of pigs, even eating the same corn as the pigs. At this absolute bottom of the pit, he has a revelation. The Gospel of Luke explains it this way.

And when he came to himself, he said,
I will arise and go to my father, and will say unto him,
Father, I have sinned against heaven, and before you,
and am no longer worthy to be called your son:
make me as one of your hired servants.
And he arose and came to his father.
But when he was yet a great way off, his father saw him,
ran to him, and fell on his neck, and kissed him.

Luke 15:17-20

The father says nothing about where he went or what he did. He asks that sandals be placed on his son's feet. "Bring a cloak and put it on him. Get a gold ring and put it on his hand. Kill the fatted calf. Call in the musicians. We're going to have a party. My son was lost, and he is found. He was dead. He has come back to life again."

God is Father-Mother to us all, and we are "forever His children." We are not simply bodies bound in space and time. All bodies die being only 'temporarily,' confined by time. Who are you when you no longer have a body, a name, and an earthly identity? Who are you when the dream is over, the legend told, the story done, the journey completed, and the dream ended? Who are you when you awaken?

Say with me:
"I am Oneself, united with my Creator."

Epistle 35

Nothing Happens by Accident

*No accident nor chance is possible within the universe
as God created it, outside of which is nothing.
Suffer, and you decided sin was your goal.
Be happy, and you gave the power of decision
to Him Who must decide for God for you.*
ACIM TEXT-21.II.3:1-6

A few years ago, I read *The Hidden Life of Trees* by Peter Wohl-leben. It's one in a series of similar books including *The Inner Life of Animals, The Secret Wisdom of Nature, The Secret Life of Plants* and *The Entangled Life.* Each of these works gives us some idea of the wide-ranging interdependency of all life, and the way in which things work together for the greater good.

Trees communicate through chemical 'sugars' released through their root system. Older trees take care of younger trees. This communication system includes all of nature, the birds and the bees, the flowers, and the trees. It includes an amazingly complex insect system, along with fungi which fall into a category somewhere between plants and animals. Interestingly, the largest living life form on earth is a honey fungus in Oregon which measures 3.4 miles across!

We have during the last few decades, become aware of some of the details of a great plan being played out in the cosmos on both a physical and psychic level. We see it in the details of our own DNA. As the Course says, *"we need to see a little in order to learn a lot."*

*There are no accidents in salvation.
Those who are to meet will meet,
because together they have the
potential for a holy relationship.
They are ready for each other.*
ACIM MANUAL FOR TEACHERS M-3.1:6-8

The phrase, God's Plan appears 46 times in the Course, primarily in reference to God's Plan for Salvation. More specifically this is the plan of the Atonement which consists, in the removal of all that we are not, so that who we are in truth, can come to the fore. As it is, we meet ourselves reflected most clearly in each other.

We see one mind being reflected in our pets, plants, and trees, in seasonal weather and in music. As Nietzsche observed, "Without music, life would be a mistake." Life is far from meaningless and the deeper we dig the more purpose and intentionality we find in all things. There is a teleological end to which every soul is persistently drawn. The ego pulls us toward "the attraction of guilt," all the while there is an even deeper pull toward "the attraction of God." Just as an iron shard cannot defy an electromagnetic field, so must we respond to the Voice for God, fulfill our destiny, and become the True Self—the Christ that we already are. It is because we are the Christ, that we must awaken to the reality our Self as the Christ.

The Bible tells us that no sparrow falls from the sky without God's knowledge. Such is the detail of our interdependence. The trick in life is to carefully follow one's own calling in conjunction with the whole of life. A good place to start is by loving everyone around you especially the ones we see the most frequently, remembering the most basic law of cause and effect. You cannot hurt someone else without hurting yourself. You cannot love someone else without loving yourself. Likewise,

You cannot but be in the right place at the right time.
Such is the strength of God. Such are His gifts.
ACIM WORKBOOK-42.2:4-6

Just as everyone's fingerprints are unique, so do each of us have a unique karmic pattern. Even though we may ignore the Voice for God, it is still there reminding us of our destiny. The important thing is to live the life we've been given as deeply as possible. Ignore the Voice for God, ignore God's plan and life will feel empty. Sing your song as brilliantly as possible remember as Thoreau said,

"Too many folks die with their music still in them."

Epistle 36

Listening to Our Inner Guide

The Holy Spirit in *A Course in Miracles*

The Voice of the Holy Spirit does not command,
because It is incapable of arrogance.
It does not demand,
because It does not seek control.
It does not overcome,
because It does not attack.
It merely reminds.
It is compelling only because
of what It reminds you "of."
ACIM TEXT-5.II.7:1-5

We avoid hearing the voice for God in much the same way as a recalcitrant adolescent shuts out his mother's voice, by setting up *an interference pattern* filled with our own static. The "noise" in our heads keeps us distracted and incapable of "hearing." The Holy Spirit thus *mediates* between the interpretations of the ego and the truth—helping us move beyond distractions by helping us *understand* the laws of God. *Understanding*, or the "light" of the Holy Spirit, can then illumine the mind—leading us to Knowledge or Heaven. Therefore, one symbol for the Holy Spirit is a flame, or light. Thus, as a little play on words, the more light there is, the "lighter" we become.

The Holy Spirit is further described in the Course as *healer, comforter, guide, mediator*, and *teacher*. Back in the mid-90's, I wrote a book titled *Listening to Your Inner Guide*. For a couple of years thereafter, I ran workshops on "Listening to Inner Guidance." In these workshops, I would ask folks to tell me about their experiences in "hearing." Some folks do report a voice coming to them so clearly that it seems auditory or maybe even extraordinary—that is, it transcends what we would think of as "normal" speech. Hearing the voice is more often simply a *clear thought* or an *insight* that you recognize as not coming from your ego's voice.

93

Lessons of the Holy Spirit

At the various workshops I have led on listening to inner guidance, I wrote down what was heard and over time collected over 200 "sayings." It was usually only a sentence or two. The most common thing that folks heard was something *comforting* as in, "I'm here to help you. Haven't I always taken care of you? I have never left you. Everything is going to be alright. You just got help." The last sentence was heard by a man who had just been fired from a job he did not enjoy. These kinds of comforting words often come when someone calls out in desperation, when they are at the bottom of the pit, when some form of disaster strikes or when they have lost someone they love, and they feel desperate.

Whatever the process, be it crashing and burning on the one extreme or quiet meditation on the other, the more we truly work on any spiritual path the more clearly and strongly the presence of the Holy Spirit is felt. The main thing is learning to quiet the ego so one can be more receptive,

Epistle 37

A New Day Dawning

Heaven is not a place nor a condition.
It is merely an awareness of perfect Oneness,
and the knowledge that there is nothing else;
nothing outside this Oneness, and nothing else within.
ACIM TEXT-18.VI.1:5-6

Since we live in space-time and our bodies are made of matter, it is difficult to imagine formlessness. Yet, spirit, love, mind, God, and life itself transcend form. Thoughts run through the mind, as electricity runs through a wire. The wire is a conduit; it is not the generator of the thought. Thoughts themselves are formless. It's what generates the thought that matters.

The body is delimited in space-time. It grows up and grows old "in time." There are levels and degrees in time. Heaven, however, being a perfected state, has no levels or degrees. Nothing is there, the Course says but that which "shines, and shines forever." Christopher Bache, Ph.D., author of *LSD and the Mind of the Universe*, describes this experience of Heaven as Diamond Luminosity. Those who have had near-death experiences or, perhaps in a meditative state achieve an experience of Heaven, inevitably say they did not want to return to bodily life. Yet, they returned for a reason; perhaps there was a child to raise or a "mission" to carry out.

Time is composed of levels and degrees. Being temporarily body bound, we are in a process of awakening. In this sense, Heaven is something we come to "realize" in time. In eternity, Heaven simply is and always has been "outside of time." Growing in time, we contract and expand, then contract and expand again—all the while moving ever deeper into a "higher" more open and expansive state. Watching cells divide, we see a turning inward and then suddenly an expansion outward. Where there was one cell, there is now two and four and eight and more—rapidly and exponentially "life" grows in form and then in knowledge which transcends form.

So much of what we hear from both mystics and scientists is that humanity is headed to a transcendence of space-time as we now understand it. God, says the Course, is the God of the Universe and the Universe of Universes. Thus, we can talk about "kinds of time," like sequential time, diurnal time, simultaneousness, and omnipresence. For everyone, there is a plan "in space-time" which is leading us Home to an awareness of Heaven. Now it seems, more than ever we are being called upon to pay attention to GPS, God's Plan for Salvation.

The soul grows (expands in knowledge and depth of awareness) via contractions and expansions and through a process of death and rebirth, then death and rebirth again, ever moving onward toward perfection. Buried inside everyone there remains "a Call to Awaken." For illustrative purposes, let's say a soul is 99% in the dark. Yet, there remains in some corner 1% of light still shining through. It remains now our responsibility to love the whole 100% regardless of the darkness within. Only love will enable that "little spark" to enliven the whole.

You are capable of enormous procrastination,
but you cannot depart entirely from your Creator,
Who set the limits on your ability to miscreate.
ACIM TEXT-2.III.3:2

With the presence of the virus, economic burdens, civil unrest, global warming, and more, we are now obviously, going through a dark time. Simultaneously, there arises new hope for a heightened "maturity" of consciousness for the whole of humankind. Even in the darkness, you can sense a new day dawning—a time for greater commitment, better communication, cooperation, and growth of spirit.

"Egos always implode." They have to. Lacking "temporarily" sufficient "spirit" within, they cannot stand, and they tumble over. While the false is exposed, love endures and finds a way. The story is told over and again. If we are paying attention; if we are looking carefully at what is happening, we can learn our way through the contractions and expansions remembering always that God is in charge, and God always prevails in the eternal now. There is just One Love, One God—right here, right now. It's simply a matter of opening one's heart and mind and letting a little light shine in, ever more enlivened by the breath of Spirit.

The Holy Spirit is the Call to awaken and be glad.
The world is very tired, because it is the idea of weariness.
Our task is the joyous one of waking it to the Call for God.

ACIM TEXT-5.II.10:5-7

Epistle 38

To See What Jesus Saw

To see what Jesus saw
is to do what Jesus did.
To let the Christ be fully known
and never hid.

To see what Jesus' saw
is to be who Jesus is.
To give our minds to Him
is to have the same as His.

To give our minds to Him
is to become the Christ as well.
To become the Christ as well
is to free of the ego's hell.

To see what Jesus' saw
is to follow the self-same path He trod.
To follow this self-same path
is to find our way to God.

To know what Jesus knows
is to be Oneself right-now.
To commit Oneself to God
is to make a solemn vow.

To follow God's Voice
this moment and forever
Is to join with kindred souls
in a beatific-great endeavor.

A friend tells of an experience one night when his wife started crying out: "Help me! Help me!" in her sleep. He turned over and, gently shaking her, he said: "Wake up, honey, you're having a bad dream." Then a few minutes later, it happened again. Realizing that he had not wakened her fully, this time he shook her more firmly and insisted that she open her eyes and look at him. Now she was fully awake. It was only a bad dream. All the while she had been safe at home in her comfy bed with her loving husband by her side. Nothing Happened!

> *You are a child of God,*
> *a priceless part of His Kingdom,*
> *which He created as part of Him.*
> *Nothing else exists and only this is real.*
> *You have chosen a sleep in which you have had bad dreams,*
> *but the sleep is not real, and God calls you to awake.*
> *There will be nothing left of your dream when you hear Him,*
> *because you will awaken.*
> ACIM TEXT-6.IV.6:1-4

The crucifixion of Jesus looks like a bad dream, but Jesus is "awake within the dream," and with this lucidity he knows that "the dreaming of the world" is not reality. He knows he is not a body, and as the Son of God he cannot be made to suffer or to die. As the last line of Martin Luther's hymn, *A Mighty Fortress* says, "The body they may kill. God's truth abideth still. His Kingdom is forever." Jesus is standing in front of Pontius Pilate, Pilate says, "Are you a king?" and Jesus says, "Yes, but my kingdom is not of this world."

Just like Jesus, we are called to awaken to the truth of who we are, not bodies trapped in time, but the sons and daughters of God forever free. We never left home. We are still resting in the arms of our Father-Mother God who loves us. There is no reason to be afraid of a dream. He has always been with us, and all we need do is to awaken to this truth. The Atonement requires a total commitment, accepting, and knowing that only Truth is True. To make the final step is to know love only and always. There is no room for fear; and there is no need to defend a non-existent ego.

> *Your resurrection is your reawakening.*
> *I am the model for rebirth,*
> *but rebirth itself is merely the dawning on your mind*
> *of what is already in it.*
> *God placed it there Himself, and so it is true forever.*
> *I believed in it, and therefore accepted it as true for me.*
> *Help me to teach it to our brothers in the name of the Kingdom of*
> *God, but first believe that it is true for you, or you will teach amiss.*
> ACIM TEXT-6.I.7:1-5

SUNDAYS WITH MUNDY

The Course reminds us that while the world may be insane, we need not be insane. To listen to the voice that Jesus heard is to be reminded of one's eternal Self.

*When you wake you will see
the truth around you and in you,
and you will no longer believe in dreams
because they will have no reality for you.
Yet the Kingdom and all that you have created there
will have great reality for you,
because they are beautiful and true.*
ACIM TEXT-6.IV.6:7-8

Epistle 39

Your Immortal Identity

Be confident that you have never lost your Identity
and the extensions which maintain It in wholeness and peace.
Miracles are an expression of this confidence.
They are reflections of both your proper identification
with your brothers, and of your awareness that
your identification is maintained by extension.
ACIM TEXT-7.IX.7:1-3

The Course makes 82 references to "Your Identity." Each time the word 'Identity' appears, the "I" is in caps as in the first sentence above. When the word 'it' (above) refers to that Identity, the "I" again is in caps. The Course also refers to "Your other Self," Your True Self, and "Your other Life" as in:

The ego is nothing more
than a part of your belief about yourself.
Your other life
has continued without interruption,
and has been and always will be
totally unaffected by your attempts to dissociate it.
ACIM TEXT-4.VI.1:6-7

To be schizophrenic means "to have a split mind." We are all schizophrenic in so far as we try to live in the world of the ego and the world of our true Identity at the same time. "You are, I am, we all are" the Christ. Only the Christ mind is true and everlasting. This is not arrogance but humility. Recognizing our Identity as the Christ we acknowledge our love of God and say, "Thy Will be done." Still, it might be best not to say you are the Christ in public, lest you be labeled schizophrenic.

We each have two lives, only one is real; the other is a dream. Our true Identity we share with the Christ mind, or Buddhahood, or Love; or call it what you will. Being beyond form, your eternal Identity has no name. All bodies obviously die. Heaven is our only eternal reality, and the body is, "the central figure in the dream."

101

Identity Crisis

To speak of our Identity is not to speak of the roles we play in time in the context of a body. We are not talking about our identity as a teacher, a pianist, a parent, a man or a woman, an Englishman or an American, etc. These words simply describe the various 'functions' we fulfill in the dreaming of the world. These functions do not speak of our Identity in Heaven. There are no Reverends in Heaven. There are no Doctors in Heaven. There is no b-o-d-y there. There are no Lieutenants, Captains, or Generals. What would we need soldiers for if there is no war?

> *It is hard to understand what*
> *"The Kingdom of Heaven is within you" really means.*
> *This is because it is not understandable to the ego,*
> *which interprets it as if something outside is inside,*
> *and this does not mean anything.*
> *The word "within" is unnecessary.*
> *The Kingdom of Heaven "is" you.*
> *What else "but" you did the Creator create,*
> *and what else "but" you is His Kingdom?*
> ACIM TEXT-4.III.1:1-5

If we go looking for Heaven in the world of things, status, pleasures of the body, we will be unfulfilled. No matter how beautiful one's surroundings, they will still be unsatisfying if the mind is not at peace. Heaven is not a place or a condition. It is an awareness of perfect Oneness and the realization that there is nothing outside of this Oneness.

Deep inside every mind is the memory of Home. That memory can never leave us. It may be blocked. It may be buried, but it is still there. In fact, its presence often haunts us, as we know on a deep, soul level that something is missing. We are being pulled as if by a magnet by "the attraction of God." We are also torn by a counter attraction which the Course calls "the attraction of guilt." This sticky seemingly-glued-on guilt is often hard to shake off. All the while, the more we are pulled by the attraction of guilt, the more we try to build our own kingdoms outside of Heaven, the deeper the guilt. The attraction of God pulls us into silent meditation, asks us to treat each other kindly, to study the Course and "inspired writings"—as we follow ever more lovingly the attraction of God, we come ever closer to knowing our Immortal Identity.

Epistle 40

Take It Deeper

Time is a trick, a sleight of hand, a vast illusion
in which figures come and go as if by magic.
Yet there is a plan behind appearances
that does not change.
The script is written.
When experience will come to end
your doubting has been set.
For we but see the journey
from the point at which it ended,
looking back on it,
imagining we make it once again;
reviewing mentally what has gone by.
ACIM WORKBOOK-158.4:1-5

Ken kindly read and offered comments on most of my books before they went to press. As I progressively sought to understand the Course, he kept saying "take it deeper." I was listening to a webinar about Ken with Judy Whitson and Diane Brook Gusic, sponsored by the Foundation for Inner peace. Diane was an 'active' student of Ken's. When she said that Ken said to her to "take it deeper," I realized he must have said the same thing to many others.

Let's take it deeper. Ultimately, there is no time. There is no past or future in eternity. In the meantime, in time, we could say that we have 'temporal' existence, but temporal is not eternal. Bodily life is completely constrained and delimited in space and time. Though we are progressively even now exponentially learning how to extend our time in the body, still time remains a limitation. There is no division into parts in eternity. There is nothing to be divided into separate parts.

The great peace of the Kingdom shines in your mind forever,
but it must shine outward to make you aware of it.
ACIM TEXT-6.II.12:8

If our "other life" is our eternal reality, then our "current life" must be seen as a dream from which there will be an awakening. As our other life is our real life. It is our real life right now. Thus, the more we can be present right now, the more our eternal reality can be seen as well. Now is as close to eternity as we can get right now. Those who have mystical experiences describe it simply as a movement more deeply than ever into the present moment. The most exciting experience we can find is that the more we get into now the more we transcend time.

The miracle is that we cannot help but be in the right place at the right time, no matter how beautiful or ugly the moment may seem to be. Heaven is here. Heaven is now. Remembering our true self is thus a complete escape from a guilt-ridden past and total freedom from a fearful future.

Anne Frank sitting in her attic prison with all hell breaking out in the world around her advises us:

Go outside, to the country,
enjoy the sun and all nature has to offer.
Go outside and try to recapture
the happiness within yourself;
think of all the beauty in yourself
and in everything around you and be happy.

Epistle 41

Living Consistently Naturally, Miraculously

Miracles are habits and should be involuntary.
They should not be under conscious control.
Consciously selected miracles can be misguided.
Miracles are natural.
When they do not occur, something has gone wrong.
Principles 5 and 6 from the 50 Principles of *A Course in Miracles*

According to the Course, the lessons we have taught ourselves have been so overlearned and fixed "they rise like heavy curtains that obscure the simple and the obvious." Thus, it is, for good or ill, we follow the mores, customs, and traditions of the 'cult,' that is, the culture into which we are born. (Cult and culture come from the same root as 'to cultivate' or 'to grow.') Unhealthy habituated patterns can become so fixed that it is hard for us to break them. Those who are prejudiced probably grew up in a prejudicial environment. Children who are overweight often have parents who are overweight. Once the habit of overeating is set, that pattern can be extremely difficult to break. There remains a host of ingrained behaviors that are incongruous with miracle-mindedness. Consequently, there is much we need to 'unlearn,' so we might then learn how to lead a truly miraculous life.

For your power to learn is strong enough to teach you that
your will is not your own, your thoughts do not belong to you,
and even you are someone else.
ACIM TEXT-31.I.3:6

Despite the training of the world, there remains a true Self that we always have been. There is a scene in the movie *Saturday Night Fever* where actor John Travolta's brother comes home to tell his parents he has given up the priesthood. In explaining himself to Travolta's character, he says of their parents, "All I ever believed in was their image of me as a priest." It is hard to awaken from a dream the world is dreaming for us. Indeed, we can only really awaken when we become aware that we are ourselves, a character within a dream. Thus, we read in the quote above: "Your thoughts do not belong to you, and even you are someone else."

Our seeing says the Course is not really 'seeing.' It is image-making. We 'make up' the world we see, by constantly evaluating the world and cultivating a particular point of view. The Course is trying to help us 'unlearn' the ways of the ego so that the loving mind of Christ can once again become, consistently, our way of seeing and thus also our home. We must first unlearn the lessons of the ego, then turn to and overlearn the way of Spirit. Overlearning is the repeated practice of a skill to strengthen memory and performance past the initial point of learning so that the neural processes involved become more efficient and recall speed improves. Thus, violinist Itzhak Perlman can say:

Amateurs practice until they get it right.
Professionals practice until they can't get it wrong.

A professional ice skater, must practice her jumps again and again, falling many times, before she can perform with precision in front of an audience. The Ten Characteristics of a Teacher of God are trust, honesty, tolerance, gentleness, joy, defenselessness, generosity, patience, faithfulness, and open-mindedness. We already possess each of these features; but we need to go deeper in cultivating these characteristics till they become habitual, natural, and so easy to practice, we do not even have to think about living miraculously. We just do it. We are then automatically patient, honest, generous, etc. We see a need; we respond to the need. We don't even have to think about it.

In this way, we begin to develop mastery; and with mastery, there comes contentment in knowing we will not fail in our mission of being mature human beings and advanced teachers of God. The Course provides us with both a text and a workbook. If the text were all we had, the Course would not be nearly as powerful as it is. We need the workbook as a training tool to live consistently—naturally—miraculously.

Epistle 42

Refusing to Accept Ourselves

Here is the end of choice.
For here we come to a decision to accept ourselves
as God created us.
And what is choice except uncertainty of what we are?
There is no doubt that is not rooted here.
There is no question but reflects this one.
There is no conflict that does not entail the single, simple question,
"What am I?"
Yet who could ask this question except one
who has refused to recognize himself?
Only refusal to accept yourself could make the question
seem to be sincere.
ACIM WORKBOOK-139.1:1-6 & 2:1-2

Ever since our separation from God, mythologically understood as the Adam and Eve story, and our decision to do things on our own, we have been in a bit of a pickle—a difficult position with, it seems, no easy answer. Unlike Heaven, which we understand as a unified state, we live with divided minds—good and bad, right, and wrong, liberal, and conservative. The choices are innumerable. The end of choice (as described in the opening sentence above) means that there is but one simple choice that can be made which will bring us back home, back to our senses, back to love, back to God and freedom from vacillation, hesitation, and uncertainty.

The "Central Teaching" of the Course is
that we have another choice.
We have chosen mistakenly and now
we can choose once again.
KEN WAPNICK

God cannot stop us in our faulty decision-making because, being part of God, we have free will. While God is not a dictator, as Lesson 138 from the Course tells us, *Heaven is a Decision I Must Make.*

To be the divine beings we always have been, we must come to

Refusing to Accept Ourselves

the "remembrance" of the truth of our being on our own. So, why don't we make this inevitable decision 'now.' Why wait for Heaven? It is here today. It is a strange conundrum that we seem to find ourselves in; for while we have free will, the fact remains that there is only one decision which will leave us finally and forever happy, namely, to reverse the ego's decision for separation and choose as Jesus did to give all to All i.e., to give our minds back to The Mind.

The Spirit that gave us Life in the first place cannot be lost. Being falsely identified with the ego, Spirit is not, within our immediate purview. While the Voice for God, is always with us, much of the time we are not paying attention. The ego is an exceptionally poor guide as it is selfish rather than selfless and it thus inevitably headed for dissolution. Thus, we often only awaken and come back to our senses after we have been through some kind of "crash and burn" experience: a divorce perhaps, bankruptcy, the loss of a job, or a health issue often brought on by our own unhealthy living.

If you listen to the wrong voice
you have lost sight of your soul.
You cannot lose it, but you cannot know it.
It is therefore "lost" to you until you choose right.
ACIM TEXT-5.II.7:12-14

There is no decision-making in Heaven. Being in a perfected state, there is no perplexity, no enigma and nothing to decide between. When only God is, only Love is. It is not a matter of right and wrong, good, and bad, love and fear. Lesson 101 from the Course is: *God's Will for Me is Perfect Happiness."* The word is "perfect." It is admittedly difficult for the ordinary (unawakened) mind to wrap itself around the idea of perfection when the ego-mind is filled with contradictions. The task of the miracle worker, says the Course, is "to deny the denial of truth."

We are simply called upon to stop listening to the ego. Stop refusing to accept yourself as you already are and always have been.

Epistle 43

Generous Out of Self Interest

The teacher of God is generous out of Self-interest.
This does not refer, however,
to the self of which the world speaks.
The teacher of God does not want anything
he cannot give away,
because he realizes it would be valueless to him by definition.
What would he want it for?
ACIM M-4.VII.2:1-4

In the first sentence above, the first word "Self" is written with a capital "S" in reference to the Christ we already are. In the second sentence, the word "self" appears with a small "s," referring to the ego, or the made-up 'self' we think we are. We are all familiar with this little self-seeking, selfish, sleeping, self—unawake and unaware of eternity, and fearful of bodily death, which it sees as its end. Simply put, there is no eternity in an ego:

You see now—here is the deal
Nothing can die that is truly real.
Seeming is not being. Seeming is dreaming.

Or to quote a famous bard:

We are such stuff as dreams are made on.
And our little life is rounded with a sleep.
'THE TEMPEST' (1611) act 4, sc. 1, l. 148

This course was sent to open the path of light to us,
and teach us, step by step,
how to return to the eternal Self we thought we lost.
ACIM WORKBOOK-reviewV.in.5:4

The ego would have us dream a dream in which we are something we are not—famous perhaps, wealthy maybe, a beauty perhaps or maybe a beast. We never quite know what mask the ego will wear. There remains a "Self" that is quite real and sane. It is this "Self" we are in truth, and this Self is the Christ.

110

The ego never gives out of abundance,
because it was made as a substitute for it.
That is why the concept of "getting"
arose in the ego's thought system.
ACIM TEXT-4.II.7:3-4

Jesus and Buddha and many thousands of unnamed souls have awakened and so can we. The Christ that enlightened them stands waiting for us to respond to a deep call from within, gently reminding us to, 'wake up,' 'get up,' and be the responsive, loving, and generous Self we are meant to be. We are generous out of Self-interest because there is only One Self. There is work to do, and we are being called to help in an inevitable great awakening, ever more clearly at hand.

If I intervened between your thoughts and their results,
I would be tampering with a basic law of cause and effect;
the most fundamental law there is.
I would hardly help you
if I depreciated the power of your own thinking.
This would be in direct opposition to the purpose of this course.
It is much more helpful to remind you that
you do not guard your thoughts carefully enough.
You may feel that at this point it would take a miracle
to enable you to do this, which is perfectly true.
ACIM TEXT-2.VII.1:4-8

The principle of generosity reflects the most fundamental law in the universe, as true in metaphysics as physics. What goes around comes around. As we give, so do we receive. A teacher of God is generous out of Self-interest. It is our job to assist "the Self" we are in our Self-Fullness.

Do all the good you can, By all the means you can,
In all the ways you can, In all the places you can,
At all the times you can, To all the people you can,
As long as forever you can.
– John Wesley (1703-1791) Founder of the Methodist Church

Epistle 44

The Practice of Patience

Patience is natural to those who trust.
Sure, of the ultimate interpretation of all things in time,
no outcome already seen or yet to come can cause them fear.
M-4.VIII.1:9–10

I had a pleasant meditation. Nothing happened. One evening, after dinner, about a half-hour before dusk; I went out onto our deck, sat down crossed-legged in a deck chair, set the time on my cell to chime in half-an-hour, and closed my eyes. Some birds were singing as they often do at twilight, and frogs were croaking in a small creek nearby. In the distance, a mile or more away, I could hear the light buzz of traffic. Then suddenly the phone made a little chime, letting me know the half-hour was gone. Where did it go? I hardly noticed its passing. I opened my eyes to see that the solar lights had come on—beautiful. You have to love it—when time stands so still that only the present is real.

Lacking patience, we believe that peace of mind depends on something external. Waiting in line is a good time to practice patience. The moment you notice impatience, say: "I could practice patience now!" A woman in a recent class told the story of finding herself on a long line at the post office with the man in front of the line taking a great deal of time with the postal clerk. Being a Course student, she decided to wait peacefully. The moment she made that decision, she said, the man at the teller's window turned, saw the long line behind him, and said to the postal clerk: "I'll return later with this; take care of these other people now." While waiting, observe your serenity and peaceful state. Patience enables awareness and attention. Take time. Look around. Patience is not simply lifeless waiting. Patience is being present and of one mind with the brothers and the sisters you see nearby.

Being patient does not mean being irresponsible, ignoring time, being lackadaisical, arriving late, or missing appointments. Living within time, we obey the laws of time, just as we obey the laws of the society of which we are a part, giving to Caesar that which is Caesar's

The Practice of Patience

and to God what is God's. If the cat doesn't go out when the door is opened for him or a child takes a long time to get ready, we can put a foot behind the cat and gently push him out the door or tell the child that we are ready to go without being the least bit upset or angry.

Complaining is nothing, fame is nothing.
Openness, patience, receptivity, solitude are everything.
Austrian Poet Rainer Maria Rilke (1875–1926)

God is infinitely patient. We wander about doing all sorts of things other than our Father's Will, yet God does not desert us nor scold us for our waywardness. The introduction to the Course says it is a required course, but the time in which we choose to do it is voluntary.

Your patience with your brother is your patience with yourself.
Is not a child of God worth patience?
I have shown you infinite patience because my will is that
of our Father, from Whom I learned of infinite patience.
His Voice was in me as it is in you, speaking for patience
towards the Sonship in the Name of its Creator.
ACIM TEXT-5.VI.11:4–7

The miracle transcends time altogether. Answers are available now, but we must be patient to see the truth. Success with the Course, as with all things, requires our "hanging in there" and remaining quiet long enough to hear the still, small Voice of God. Only when we are non-projective do we experience real peace of mind. Stillness has no place to go.

Patience waits for the right time, the right principle, and the right way. It understands that everyone fails, and it sees no benefit in rushing. When a mistake is made, patience allows time to correct the error. Patience, says the Course, is natural to the teacher of God. Patience gives us the ability to hold on in difficult times.

Epistle 45

God Cannot Judge

Judgment is not an attribute of God.
ACIM TEXT-2.VIII.2:3

Love cannot judge.
As it is one itself, it looks on all as one.
Its meaning lies in oneness.
And it must elude the mind that thinks of it as partial or in part.
There is no love but God's, and all of love is His.
There is no other principle that rules where love is not.
Love is a law without an opposite.
ACIM WORKBOOK-127.3:1-7

Is there anything God cannot do? Yes, God cannot not be God. As this sentence contains a double negative, the second 'not' cancels the first. The Course, like every enduring spiritual path, says that God is love. It also says that Love does not condemn. Therefore, the only correct response is always love. God is love, and the Course also says that God is life. Thus, life is love, and love is life. To know God is to be immersed in love and therefore in life. The more awake we are, the more alive we are, the more in love we are. Love reaches to everything created like itself. It is completely impartial in its giving. Nineteen different times, the Course says: "God cannot," as in:

God cannot be out of accord with Himself,
and you cannot be out of accord with Him.
ACIM TEXT-7.V.6:14

To be out of accord with the Mind of God is to be unhappy.
As no one wants to be unhappy, the only solution is to choose to keep
one's mind aligned with the One Mind of God.
Only in this way can we know contentment and peace.
For the memory of God can dawn only in a mind that
chooses to remember, and that has relinquished the
insane desire to control reality.
ACIM TEXT-12.VIII.5:3

God Cannot Judge

Let's say you are introduced to someone new. The minute that happens, any one of us will make several judgments. First, there are physical differences. This person is tall, short, or average height. This person is intelligent, attractive, or unattractive; old or young; witty or dull, and the list goes on. The thing about all these judgments is that they don't make any difference—unless we think they do. Let's be grateful then for 'black lives matter,' for LGBTQ, and those expansions in consciousness that allow for differences without making differences matter. My darling Dolores has said that her favorite line from the Course is,

> *Let him be what he is, and seek not to make of love an enemy.*
> ACIM TEXT-19.IV.D.13:8

Let her be who she is. Let him be who he is. Let 'it,' the situation, be what it is. If you are stuck in traffic, do you want to lose your peace of mind? Or can you maintain your serenity in the face of what you see in front of you? This traffic is probably not going to move for a while. In this situation, I can go crazy and lose my peace of mind, or I can hold to the center of my Being and remain at peace. Which way will it be? God does not condemn, and neither can the Christ in you.

> *The Christ in you can see your brother truly.*
> *Would you decide against the holiness He sees?*
> ACIM TEXT-24.VI.10:1-8

> *The Christ in you is very still.*
> *He knows where you are going,*
> *and He leads you there in gentleness and blessing all the way.*
> ACIM TEXT-24.V.6:1-2

Epistle 46

Disciplining the Mind

You want to be happy. You want peace.
You do not have them now,
because your mind is totally undisciplined,
and you cannot distinguish between
joy and sorrow, pleasure and pain, love and fear.
You are now learning how to tell them apart.
And great indeed will be your reward.
ACIM WORKBOOK-20.2:3-8

The word discipline comes from the Latin *disciplina*, meaning "teaching," "learning," or "knowledge." It has the same root as disciple, meaning "student," or "follower." A student follows a specific discipline to learn a specific subject or develop a specific skill, as in the discipline it takes to learn to play a musical instrument. In like manner, it takes discipline to study the Course and receive from it, its great reward—"peace of mind." The more unhappy we are, the more 'unlearning' we must do. Yes, the word is 'unlearning.' It's the big belly and the angry attitude that we want to be free of, and that takes discipline.

Only the hand which erases, writes the right thing.
German Mystic Meister Eckhart (1260—1328)

The good news is that when we apply ourselves and do what we are being asked to do, we feel good about ourselves. How much time is given to compulsions, to hungers of the body we "seem" unable to control? And who is the 'we' who cannot control it? Are you not the overseer of your mind?

True discipline comes in remembering what we really want and making a commitment to it. It's actually easier to do what God is asking us to do than it is to resist and follow our own (the ego's) will. We know when we're giving in to the ego. We know when we're overeating. We know when we're getting angry. We know when we're about to say something we will regret, so why do we do it? Just a little discipline is needed. It's fun and easy to study this Course, to exercise, to do some yoga, to go for a walk. It's also easy not to do it, and that is the difference between success and failure.

116

Disciplining the Mind

Increasing discipline in one area of life enhance our ability to be more disciplined in another area. The more disciplined I am in eating healthy, the more discipline I can have in studying, cleaning, in paying attention to the needs of my friends and family. Move; put the feet on the floor. Take the first step. Do what God is asking you to do, and don't say you don't know what it is.

The basic decision of the miracle-minded is
not to wait on time any longer than is necessary.
Time can waste as well as be wasted.
The miracle worker, therefore,
accepts the time-control factor gladly.
ACIM TEXT-1.V.2:1-3

Everything affects everything else. All disciplines affect each other. Everything matters: every action, every attack thought, and every expression of love matters. Practice the discipline of doing the daily lesson in the Course, and you may find the time to do a 10-minute meditation as well. Being disciplined helps us to feel good about ourselves. Then it feels as though we're moving in the right direction. It's easy to complain about politicians and the affairs of the world but what benefit is it? There is a saying:

If you do what is easy, your life will be hard.
If you do what is hard, your life will be easy.

The Course is asking us to take back our minds. The ego has been in charge long enough. Let's give our minds to God to guide. If we do, we'll be rewarded over and over, time and again. Give the mind to Spirit, and there will be a different and much more satisfying result.

Your mission is very simple.
You are asked to live so as
to demonstrate that you are not an ego,
and you do not choose God's channels wrongly.
ACIM TEXT-4.VI.6:2-3

Epistle 47

What is Temptation?

What is temptation but a wish to make illusions real?
ACIM TEXT-30.VIII.3:1

A temptation is a distraction. It is a form of self-indulgence that attracts the mind and keeps us blind. It is a decision to be something we are not, to be a wayward son or daughter. Temptation is a wish to create our own world, to be the king, the queen, the monarch, the mighty sovereign, and ruler of the world we see. "I want ice cream. A little never hurt." But then, of course, a little and a little, and a little make a lot.

> *Today I learn the law of love; that what I give my brother*
> *is my gift to me. This is Your law, my Father, not my own.*
> *I have not understood what giving means, and thought to*
> *save what I desired for myself alone.*
> ACIM WORKBOOK-344

Temptations pull us from our path and draw us in if and only if we ourselves give in. Temptations, even little things, pull us away from God, away from love and all we really are. The problem in going off on our own. It is the futility of attempts at self-creation.

> *Some forms of idols have a powerful appeal that makes*
> *them harder to resist than those you would not want to*
> *have reality. Temptation, then, is nothing more than this;*
> *a prayer the miracle touch not some dreams, but keep their*
> *unreality obscure and give to them reality instead.*
> ACIM TEXT-30.VIII.3:2-3

No matter what Illusions we may choose, an illusion is an illusion, and will never bring anything but illusion. It will pull us into lonely self-centeredness. In saying no we choose a path of liberty and confidence that comes in making every decision, even small ones in alignment with the laws of God.

When the temptation to attack rises
to make your mind darkened and murderous,
REMEMBER
you "can" see the battle from above.
Even in forms you do not recognize,
the signs you know.
There is a stab of pain, a twinge of guilt,
and above all, a loss of peace.
This you know well.
When they occur leave not your place on high,
but quickly choose a miracle instead of murder.
ACIM TEXT-23.IV.6:1-5

Lesson 193 from the Course tells us, *All things are lessons God would have me learn.* Temptations are lessons too, insofar as they help us realize and with clarity, what we do not want and do not need. We are called upon to say "yes" to that which gives us Life and "no" to that which would encumber our awakening and diminish awareness of Heaven. Overcoming limits makes us stronger. Some of the folks who participate in Alcoholics Anonymous are students of the Course and the principles for correction are much the same, namely taking full responsibility for our actions and ceasing to engage in choices that hurt rather than help us.

What is temptation
but a wish to make the wrong decision
on what you would learn, and
have an outcome that you do not want?
You are deceived if you believe
you want disaster, disunity, and pain.
Hear not the call for this within yourself.
ACIM TEXT-31.1:11:1-3

Temptations lead to 'rewards' we do not want. A major temptation that everyone can relate to is the temptation to over-eat. According to the Centers for Disease Control, 74 percent of adults in the United States are now overweight. That includes 43 percent who are obese. The choice of what, when, and how much to eat is ours to make—can we make the healthy choice?

Each day, each hour and minute, even each second,
you are deciding between the crucifixion and the resurrection;
between the ego and the Holy Spirit.
The ego is the choice for guilt;
the Holy Spirit the choice for guiltlessness.
The power of decision is all that is yours.
ACIM TEXT-14.III.4:1-3

Say with me:
In me, salvation's means and end are one.

Epistle 48

Love Your Story

You will undertake a journey
because you are not at home in this world.
And you will search for your home
whether you realize where it is or not.
If you believe it is outside you the search will be futile,
for you will be seeking it where it is not.
ACIM TEXT-12.IV.5:1-3

The body is a figure in a dream, and every dream tells a story of awakening. Thus, how we dream our dream or live our story, determines our contentment or our desolation. Will it be a happy dream, or must I wander about in a seeming nightmare? We're on a journey, looking to find the Buddha, the Christ, the Self within and thus a place where there is no sin. The good news is that Self has already been found. Even if we're not aware of the search, it remains alive inside, like an underground stream gently carrying us home.

What will happen in our dream? Will our journey be smooth—or will we encounter demons and dragons of our own making? How deeply and clearly will we respond to the call? Will we succeed or will we fall? And if we fall, can we get up and begin again? Eventually, the Course tells us we all make it Home; in other words, we all awaken. In the meantime:

Attitude is everything,
and
altitude determines attitude.

The hope of peace is never found on a bloody battleground. There is no one here who will not be tried and repeatedly. Awakening is dependent on our acknowledging that the dream we find ourselves is a classroom of our own choosing.

Remember that no one is where he is by accident,
and chance plays no part in God's plan.
It is most unlikely that changes in attitudes would not be
the first step in the newly made teacher of God's training.
M-9.1:3-4

Let me not see my dream as a frightening thing, but a game that happy children play designed by One Who loves His children, and Who would replace fearful toys with joyous games, which teach us that the game of fear is gone. When a divorce, a bankruptcy, an illness, a job lost, or the death of a loved one comes our way, will I crumble? Will I attack my ex? Will I blame someone else for my condition? Can I face this downward turn in life and look to see—what is the lesson it has for me? Can I love even through tragedy? We are called to transcend the insanity of the world. We are called upon to be 'responsible' journeyers. We may not remember the moment in which it happened, but we chose to be here—in this incredible jungle, at this wondrous time. Lesson 253 asks us to say to ourselves:

It is impossible that anything should come to me
unbidden by myself.
Even in this world, [this dream] it is I who rule my destiny.
What happens is what I desire.
What does not occur is what I do not want to happen.
This must I accept.
ACIM WORKBOOK-253.1:1-4

If you get Covid or any disease—you might say, "I didn't ask for this." Sometimes diseases are clearly of our own making. If I smoke, overeat, or drink too much—I plainly choose my malady. When a disease comes from the outside, our choosing it is not so clear. Nevertheless, If I have it, I must have asked for it. Lesson 31 reads:

"I am not a victim of the world I see."

Epistle 49

Ain't Gonna Study War No More

The means of war are not the means of peace,
and what the warlike would remember is not love.
ACIM TEXT-23.I.1:3

Anger is "never" justified. Attack has no foundation.
ACIM TEXT-30.VI.1:1-2

One of the simplest ways to practice the principles of the Course is to never attack anyone for any reason ever in thought, word, or deed! Remember:

If you attack error in another, you will hurt yourself.
ACIM TEXT-3.III.7:

The Course is asking us to become more conscious, more aware of our own insanity, let that go (forgiveness is the key), and then move on in love. A good place to start is by the simple process of looking at the words that come out of our mouths and their intention. Where do the words I'm using come from? Why am I speaking about this topic? What is the objective? How much time do I spend judging the world I see? I was listening to someone speaking who kept using the word 'terrible.' Terrible is a heavy word. When socializing notice: Do I feel compelled to share my judgments? How much do I engage in complaining, attack, fault-finding, and gossip?

We are at all times either choosing out of love or fear. To choose out of fear is to choose from ego. (Spirit knows there is nothing to fear.) If I choose out of love, whatever I experience I cannot but be happy. Which way would you like to go? Practicing the Course means growing in Love.

The most telling and profound way of describing the evolution of
the universe would undoubtedly be to trace the evolution of love.
Father Pierre Teilhard de Chardin (1881-1955)

SUNDAYS WITH MUNDY

For several years during the 1970s, I taught a class titled "Jung, Chardin and The Future of Consciousness" at the New School University in NYC. Teilhard was a Jesuit priest, scientist, and paleontologist who held that an evolution in consciousness is pulling everyone ever more deeply into Love or what he called the Omega Point, i.e., everything in the universe is spiraling toward a final point of unification. In Course terms, Oneness.

More recently, Stephen Pinker, Ph.D., professor of psychology and linguistics at Harvard, in his book *The Better Angels of our Nature* points out that, since 1990, more than 1.2 billion people have risen out of extreme poverty. As a species, we are becoming more mature and more willing to help rather than to hurt each other.

Gonna Lay Down My Sword and Shield

I believe, as did Chardin, that we are headed in an ever-inward expansion in consciousness brought on by our ability to become intentionally more aware of our own insanity and "stop it," in favor of more loving communication and thus communion. We engage in this communion by seeing all things from a non-judgmental, non-attacking, non-defensive point of view. There is no one we want to attack. If our desire is only to love, our experience will be one of being loved.

Salvation . . . merely asks that you respond appropriately
to what is not real by not perceiving what has not occurred.
ACIM TEXT-30.VI.2:5

Let's say that you experience yourself being attacked verbally. To respond to an attack by attacking back is simply to compound and aggravate the situation amplifying the illusion.

Teach no one he has hurt you, for if you do,
you teach yourself that what is not of God has power over you.
ACIM TEXT-14.III.8:2

Epistle 50

I Am Not a Body!?!

Note: the following piece was written after my returning home from 24 days in the hospital with Covid in the summer of 2021.

Bodies are delimited by space and time; and when space and time end for anyone, so does the body and the world. For this reason, the Course says, "there is no world." If you're not in the world, is there a world? Maybe it's all a dream or maybe as Marilyn Monroe said, "It's all make-believe, isn't it?"

Miracles reawaken the awareness that the spirit,
not the body, is the altar of truth.
ACIM Miracles Principal No. 26

Anandamayi Ma, (1896-1981) a highly respected Hindu mystic said that she had become empty with no sense of "I am." She would objectify her body when speaking about herself saying. "This body went there, or this body did such and such." Egos are bodily based, and we would find that way of speaking awkward and yet humor me for a moment.

This body returned to its home this last week having spent 24 days in a sealed room at our regional hospital where it engaged in a wrestling match with two diseases Babesiosis, a disease transmitted via deer ticks, which attacks one's red blood cells, and Covid. Covid took the upper hand and led me into many restless days and nights. On perhaps the worst day, I awoke to find the body reduced to skin and bones and in a fetal position. This was also the day I decided that while…

Tolerance for pain may be high, it is not without limit.
Eventually everyone begins to recognize, however dimly,
that there "must" be a better way.
As this recognition becomes more firmly established,
it becomes a turning point.
ACIM TEXT-2.III.5-7

… I had to start getting better. While physical therapy was supposed to be part of the plan of recovery, I had only received one short visit from a physical therapist. So, I persuaded a nice nurse named

125

Genene to begin helping me try to walk around in the room three or four times each day.

Then there was another kind of healing. All I had with me was my cell phone with a recording of the Course and a long weekend recording of Ken Wapnick on *Living A Course in Miracles*. Here was Ken helping me once again saying take it deeper. As my friend Bonnie Nack said in a recent email, "I find that as I read the Course these days, it means so much more to me than it did twenty years ago." It's possible to hear the Course on many different levels; and, My God, this Course is deep. It's going all the way Home and will take us with it if we are willing.

As part of the journey, I found myself engaging in several early morning "life reviews," looking at more guilt than I would normally allow into a busy, everyday, consciousness. While this was not fun, it proved restorative. Then, too, there came wonderful non-evaluative blank, empty states -- what perhaps Einstein meant by "swimming in silence" freed from the burden of words.

I had a post-hospital Zoom meeting with my GP. He studied my charts from the hospital for a few minutes and then he said: "You are lucky to be alive." He said the same thing in 2007 after I awoke from a week of being in a coma brought on by the bite of a mosquito thus inducing "viral La Cross encephalitis." Encephalitis was different from Covid. It was not painful, as I was in a coma; and I awoke in a very childlike state, at first not even knowing who I was or being able to talk. Very slowly, I began to put the pieces of this world back together while thankfully maintaining a transcendent perspective.

Why did this happen? I don't know. Why did Ken Wapnick die at the age of only 71? I tend to agree with Roman Emperor and Stoic Philosopher Marcus Aurelius (121-180) when he writes in his *Meditations*, "All things happen as they should." Or, as the Course says, *The impossible can happen only in fantasy.* T-9.IV.11.1. Was this then all a fantasy? The further we move in time away from such experiences, the more that seems to be true. This much I do know.

I am responsible for what I see.
I choose the feelings I experience,
and I decide upon the goal I would achieve.
And everything that seems to happen to me I ask for,
and receive as I have asked.

ACIM TEXT-21.II.2:3-5

Epistle 51

"Being"
Who We Are Meant "To Be"

Spirit is in a state of grace forever.
Your reality is only spirit.
Therefore, you are in a state of grace forever.
ACIM TEXT-1.III.5:1-6

Make sure you understand the fundamental principles of the
trunk and the big branches before you get into the leaves.
ELON MUSK

Your Reality Is Only Spirit

Who does not think about their death? Who are you without a body? The Course is trying to help us move from illusion to truth. Thus, lesson 97 from the Course affirms: "I am spirit."

We thank our Father for one thing alone;
that we are separate from no living thing,
and therefore, one with Him
ACIM WORKBOOK-195.6:1

All of 'life' is imbued with spirit. Animals are often more comfortably, instinctively, and more securely centered in their bodies and in line with the Will of God than are we. Dogs are indeed God spelled backward. Animals think and feel, but they do not think about thinking and feeling. Humans are capable of self-reflective thought. We not only think, but we also think about thinking. We are in this sense, subject to time—every second of it. What kind of decisions do we make in time? We are at liberty to choose, in every second, how we will respond to our thoughts and to the world around us; and in this, we open the door to 'misthought'.

The body can act wrongly only
when it is responding to misthought.
The body cannot create, and the belief that it can,
a fundamental error, produces all physical symptoms.
ACIM TEXT-2.IV.2:5-6

127

This is a course in mind training, and we are being led ever so gently to make a better choice. This time even more deeply in alignment with 'the Mind of God.' All life is interconnected: the flowers, the trees, the bacteria, bushes, birds, and bees. Being in nature automatically gives us a sense of interconnectedness. The same is true for music, the visual arts, dancing, and falling in love. In these ways and a myriad more, we are assured of our present and eternal reality.

As God's creative Thought proceeds from Him to you,
so must your creative thought proceed
from you to your creations.
Only in this way can all creative power extend outward.
ACIM TEXT-7.I.2:3-4

Creative Thoughts

God has given us the power not only of thought but "creative thought." Creative thought gives us the opportunity to extend love, at all times and in all places. What an easy job and how rewarding. We have within us the same 'Loving Will to Create' as that of our Father. Extending love is the most exciting thing we can do. When we do it, we are spontaneously filled with purpose, energized, and able to do even more—and cover all we see with love.

To extend is a fundamental aspect of God
which He gave to His Children. In the creation,
God extended Himself to His creations
and imbued them
with the same loving Will to create.
You have not only been fully created,
but have also been created perfect.
ACIM TEXT-2.I.1:1-3

To be imbued means to be instilled, infused, impregnated, and permeated with the Love of God. We cannot ask for anything better than that. It is what happens every time we fall in love, regardless of what or with whom we fall in love: be it music, nature, art, writing, building, gardening, an animal or another human being. We are here to be generative—each of us contributing in our own unique way to loving the world we see—and letting life simply be. Could it get any easier or better than that?

Say with me

Fear binds the world. Forgiveness sets it free.
The ego makes illusions.
Truth undoes the ego's evil dreams by shining them away.

Epistle 52

God Is Life

Life is as holy as the Holiness by which it was created.
The Presence of Holiness lives in everything that lives,
for Holiness created life,
and leaves not what It created holy as Itself.
ACIM TEXT-14.IX.4:5-6

In early 2022, I taught a class on "Romanticism, American Tran-scendentalism, Christian Science, The New Thought Movement, and A Course in Miracles." It was fun reviewing these schools of thought and I would enjoy doing it again in greater depth. In study-ing these different disciplines, you can see how one grew out of the other each one adding something 'new' to what came before.

As God is Love and God is Life,
so, Love is Life and Life is Love.

As love is an experience, so God is an experience. Indeed, God is not something other than who we are right now when we are awake to that knowledge.

Very early on I knew
the only object in life was to grow.
American Transcendentalist,
Margaret Fuller (1810-1850)

As we study the Transcendentalist and the New Thought think-ers, we meet people who sought to be in love with life by being in love with God.

I went to the woods
because I wanted to live deliberately,
to confront the essentials of life
and not when I came to die discover I had not lived.
American Transcendentalist
Henry David Thoreau (1817-1862)

One thing that can never be taken away from us is the Love of God and, the deeper we go in Loving God (by loving all of life), the more God can open the door to His love for us.

The thief (the ego) comes to steal,
and to kill, and to destroy:
I am come that you might have life,
and that they might have it more abundantly.
Jesus speaking in John 10:10

While *ultimately*, we are not a body, *temporarily* – in this moment in space-time—we each have a body. What will we do with it? The best thing we can do with this tool is to appreciate it, keep it in good repair and use it to grow in depth of understanding and awareness.

Life does not sit still—it just keeps growing -- and as it grows so is the meaning of life revealed. Time and again a shell is broken, and new life emerges. It is true physically, mentally, and spiritually. What happens physically is only an external manifestation. The old die so something new can be born. Churches are dying and changing. We still need to be able to hug each other, to pray and sing together, and care for each other directly. At the same time something new is being born, something unbounded by walls or even geography. It is happening right now in every heart, in every woman, and every man. And it is happening on our computers, as they stretch around the land.

We are here to 'love living' and in living life grow ever more deeply in love. When Covid slowed everything down in the outside world so that inside the Mind there could be a gestation; an incubation and maturation could occur for all of us. This gestation has been happening for a long time, and it is getting more exciting. It is an experience, just like love is an experience, and it is delicious, palpable, and profound.

Religion is experience;
psychotherapy is experience.
At the highest levels they become one.
ACIM Psychotherapy 2.II.2:2-3

Religions and psychotherapy are one because psychotherapy and religion, are 'healing balms.' They are the processes by which we can be changed and the old turned into fertile soil. Digging ever deeper into life, we are given the opportunity to grow in love with God, and each other and therein discover ever more about the Christ within. To be the Christ, we need to be loving life ever more consistently and more deeply, which means 'loving' everything: the screaming child, the nagging partner, the disagreeable co-worker, and the 'unpleasant task.' Vietnamese Buddhist master Thich Nhat Hanh suggests turning 'doing the dishes' into a meditation.

God is an experience.
Love is an experience. Life is an experience.
Our objective is to live life in love.
That is the only way it has ever been or can be.

Dance, sing, do yoga, walk, swim, read, write, study, play
and live life fully another day.

God is here and God will take care of you.

PART II

Jon's Poems

Embracing the Christ

God wants to speak to you.
Are you willing to let him thru?
His voice is loving. His message kind.
There is something important He has in mind.

Why this recalcitrance, this stubborn obstinacy,
this lack of willingness to do what is right?
Why put up such an enduring fight?

Like a caring parent at your bedroom door,
His message is simple; and what is more,
It will lift your Spirit and bring relief,
And free you from your nagging grief.

God loves you for the truth in you –
Your power and strength—if you only knew.
You've been distracted by the ego for far too long.
Only Spirit can make you strong.

Rise up and wipe away your tears,
And give God all your useless fears.
So, what if you've been wrong.
There is work to do that will make you strong.

Maple Seeds and Seraphim

The angels are dancing out in the sky.
Comes a gust of a wind and oh how they fly.

All about -- they play with the wind.
Whirling and twirling, they slowly descend.

Ballerinas with wings, they twist, and they twine.
They turn on one toe. They seem quite divine.

They come out of the branches, high up in the leaves.
They land on my shirt and slide down my sleeves.

The sun is a shinning, and the source is quite clear.
They come from the maple trees standing so near.

The dappling sun makes it a magnificent sight,
as they swivel and dance and play in the light.

How nimble they are. How graceful the dance.
They offer a wink and a little romance.

Their life is so brief. It last just so long.
They must reach earth before they sing out their song.

You see, each ballerina is pregnant at birth,
but cannot deliver unless she finds earth.

Inside each one is an entire maple tree.
How amazingly condensed Mother Nature can be.

The squirrels are elated—manna's at hand
as the next one, and next one, and next one yet lands.

Thousand and thousand, they all now descend,
an abundant supply: they come without end.

So, if they are lucky and the squirrels do not see,
soon standing before you is a small maple tree.

Where Is Forgiveness?

Sin and attack go fist in hand,
Across a dry and arid land.
Attack and sin are "tit for tat,"
Or so it is a "this for a that."

You have sinned -- I can straighten you out.
And so, we throw insults about.
I know so clearly where the fault does lie.
And the solution is -- that you must die!

Your puny ego does not take this well.
And now it seems -- we're both in hell.
And so, these days -- we are at war,
To settle an uneven score.

I attack you. You attack me.
And long we languish in a bloody sea.
I lose an eye and you a tooth.
And still, we both avoid the truth.

My brother has so many sins
That no one, no one -- ever wins.
Around and around and around we go
and where's forgiveness?
Does anyone know?

Vision Is No Idle Gift

Mind is far beyond time.
In time there is a climb.
In time there is a hustle.
In time It's a struggle.

But
When you get to the top
-- you can stop.
When you get to the top
-- you can see.
At the top you have vision
and no indecision.
-- at the top you can just let things be.

At the top it is perfectly clear.
Now truth and love can appear
In all their beauty.
You know it's your duty
To reach down and draw others up near.

When you get to the top,
 there is a breeze.
When you get to the top,
you can fall on your knees.
And thank God Almighty
 for His help on the way.
And for-giving you a place,
where you can just—sit—stay.

At the top it's all mighty fine.
At the top does the light ever shine.
At the top there is a view.
I would share it with you.

This moment is perfect
 made by design.
There just one of us here.
What is yours is what's mine.
Call it Home. Call it Heaven.
Or just Peace of Mind.

Love Always Wins

Love always wins.
It always gets you in the end,
back at the point before time begins.

This Course is quite guileless,
The message most clear.
There is nothing to fear.

The body will end. That is a given.
There is no eternity here,
but it's a definite in Heaven.

The laws of eternity are not those of time.
All is God-given. There is no mountain to climb.
There is no eye for an eye, or tooth for a tooth,
All that is needed is the simple truth.

We Really Love Each Other!

That is the only way anything ever can be!
No matter where we are standing,
No difference the Holy See.

There is no reason -- to block God's way
Alpha and omega are here to stay.
All we need do, is not interfere.
Love is a given, simple, and clear.

To give is to recognize - you have received.
And to prove what it is - that you believe.

The world is a confusion, a division at best,
A place where the ego knows nothing of rest.
Heaven is knowing -- we are already home.
There is no separation and no reason to roam

There is no buying in Heaven,
No property division—and no acquisition.
We simply hold to a unified vision.
All Power is of God's
And to Us, All Power is Given.

Perfect Happiness Now

A day of grace is given me
And now I do clearly see it.

There is a light my eyes see not
And yet my mind beholds it.

Now do I see there is no loss
When I have left illusion

The world holds nothing that I want
And so, my choice is clear.

I find it not by leaving here
But in The Mind—Eternal.

There is a place of timelessness,
Where love endures forever.

Here losing is impossible.
And vengeance has no meaning.

Here God speaks clearly to his Child.
And now his Child does answer.

God's Will is perfect happiness
Why choose against Myself?

God's Will is perfect happiness
For all sisters and all brothers.

God wills is perfect happiness
For all who will declare it.

There is now nothing left to find
Perfection has been given.

I move now forward Home to God.
Now is the last step certain.

Adam's Love Song

Perhaps we'll meet again someday.
perhaps in a beautiful garden.
Maybe, we won't be alone anymore.
Maybe, we'll be back together.
Maybe, we won't need these clothes anymore.
Maybe, we won't have these bodies.
Maybe, none of that matters.
Maybe, we're a thought in the Mind of God.
Maybe, we're a Ray of Light.
Maybe, we Last Forever.

These Summer Evenings

Sitting—outside on a summers evening.
After—a hard day of 'bucking bails.'
Our barn—now filled with hay.
Our bellies—full of mother's supper.
My father—smoking a cigar.
Talking—about nothing consequential.
Sometimes—not talking at all.
Sitting—watching evening fall.
Listening—to the katydids, tree frogs and crickets.
A lite breeze—rustles the leaves.
And then—the stars, the moon and the fireflies.
Sleep—comes so peacefully – these summer evenings.

My Experience with Covid

I decided to look and see
What kind of gift, it had for me?
And thus, I laid awake one night
turned and looked for an inner light.
There is so much to love here every day
even the pain that comes our way.

Jesus asks us to love it all
the exciting triumph and the disastrous fall.
Love your wonderful nagging wife,
no matter what the seeming strife.
Love the taxes you must pay
and all the blessings they bring your way.

Love the one who does not work as hard as you.
And remember he is your brother too.
Love the moon, and stars at night.
And in the morning the returning light.

Pray for the Trout

There are a lot of fly fishermen today
Standing in the water.
clear up to their knees
down on the Delaware River.

The trout don't have much of a chance, I think.
They are not very safe in the shallows.
Next thing you know there is a "bling, bling,"
and a cute little bug with a hook in its butt
is sitting on top of the water.

Trout are a lot like human's ya know.
before long, your appetite gets ya.
and then you spend the rest of ya life,
a fighting' for your life,
clear up past the surface.
all the way back to the Kingdom of Heaven.

Once upon a tiny tick in time,

There came a thought into the mind.
There came a supposition.
Nothing more than a miniscule cognition.
A rumor rolled around inside the mind,
Like many a myth, which makes us blind.
A fantasy, a wisp of wit,
Lead to a most incredible split.
What if it was possible to pull-off a fantastic fraud?
What if I can think a thought outside of the mind of God?

Hatred Is Forgotten

Is it not insane to offer thanks?
because another suffers more?
Or think that it is good
because men go to war?

There is no place to hide –
no place where we can run.
We have a blessed function here –
to become at last just One.

We can escape our prison –
though we thought it lacked a door.
When love is found at last –
and we know of nothing more.

A brother is an enemy –
only if I see a rival.
The only way out is loving him –
in this is our survival.

We offer thanks to God
when all men find their freedom.
And we learn at last
We share His perfect Kingdom.

Make room for those who escape with you:
the anxious and afraid,
the sick, the weak, the needy,
the despairing, and dismayed.

And those who mourn a seeming loss
or feel apparent pain,
who suffer cold or hunger,
or think they live in vain.

Let us no longer condemn, nor think
the less of those who think we are not One.
Or think that we have sins
for which we must atone.
While in Truth we are God's Son.

We cannot retain some things
still locked away as "sins."
And only escape
when everybody wins.

Love makes no comparisons
and gratitude is part of love –
when we know that all we have
comes to us from up above.

Let our brothers lean their weary heads
upon our welcoming shoulders.
And may we all find rest
as enmity no more smolders.

Let us be free of this insane world
where all is ever erratic.
The fear of God is undone at last,
and forgiveness automatic.

An ancient door swings free.
And a long forgotten Word
re-echoes in our memory.

Today we think of gratitude
in place of malice and revenge.
And what had hurt us once
will hurt us not again.

No one can gain freedom,
while another remains bound.
Where love is there,
gratitude is also found.

Your gratitude to Him
is one with His to you.
God loves us always –
there's nothing else for Him to do.

Now do I let all vengeance go –
now would I be set free.
And would I forgive
the sins of all humanity.
Hatred is forgotten
when comparisons are laid aside.
And all thoughts of attack
have finally, finally, died.

As You Decide, So Will You See

Turn on the news and see what has unfurled.
It is easy to find problems, in this worn and weary world.
We do it all the time, and it's easy to do.
You can always find some problems staring back at you.
Yet, is it not more fun to be the love we are
Than to go looking for sin in a friend, acquaintance, or star?
Through the eyes of Christ, only the real world can be seen.
Or is it more important, what's in the current scene?

PART III

Jon's Sayings

Rhyme Lines

If on my brother's sins I dwell,
I seek to send us both to hell.
When I forgive,
we are both set free
and we know again eternity.

Nothing lasting lies in dreams
or any of the ego's schemes

Jesus is quietly busy,
talking specifically
 to everyone,
and creatures – many more,
All things are the same to him.
He has walked
this road before.

The sense of sin inside of me
Does not like the world I see.
Convicted now, I'm filled with sin,
I cannot see, the Christ within.

Dogmas, doctrines,
laws, and creeds
confine the mind
 and confuse our needs.
So do miracles set us free
enabling sight of eternity.

When I lose the fear
 of Love, I see
It's right here in front of me.

The self-deceived receive deception.
Hell is but a chain reaction.

In even the simplest fairy tale,
some problem must prevail.

There is something
greater than we can see
surpassing all definition of
"you" and "me."

Bodies are made of matter.
Nobody lasts
and it doesn't matter.

How many souls are lost
in some drama,
some romance gone wrong,
some somebody done gone
and done me wrong song?

How can I have a point of view
If all I ever see is me?
or
How can you have
a point of view
if the only thing you see,
is you?

I am tired of fighting Spirit
Spirit always wins.
With this kind of luck
I think I'll just give in.

When we can get the mind
to be still—we see.
We always have been.
We always will be.

Heaven is here. Heaven is now.
It is the only place we can ever be
and also know eternity.
All sickness is homesickness.
We're always headed home.

The world "I think 'I' see" is clearly not reality.
The past only exists in the present if I hold on to it.

Mysticism

When it comes to mysticism,
a lot can be said about what cannot be said.
Mysticism is non-nihilistic negativity or
all there is, is God.

Mysticism is quite natural.
It is in fact, is the most natural thing of all.
Solitary mystics are the most connected individuals.

The practical mystic keeps her eyes
on Heaven and her feet on the ground.

Quiet, Meditation

In wonder and awe
we praise God without words

Be quiet for a while
and you can hear
the whisper of God
upon your ear.

If you love
the way you are living,
if you are listening to and following the Voice for God
then you are living a miraculous life.

If you are going through hell
You're having a bad dream.
Dreams end when we awaken.

Falling in love
is remembering oneness.

After a lifetime of trying,
tyrants must with sadness realize that there is
no world to possess.

Forgiveness

Condemn and
be made a prisoner.
Forgive and be set free.

Forgiveness does not keep time. It ends it.
God has already forgiven you for all the things you did not do.

There is nothing to forgive
unless I think there is.

The less I mess with the world,
the less it messes with me.

Forgiving ourselves
we are set free
And remember again eternity.

Depression is derived
from Self-deprivation.

Projection and Perception
Illusion and the Dreaming of the World

What do you lose when you lose an illusion?
In order to see, close your eyes.

Awakening always means
"we were" dreaming.

It is not what we look at that matters,
It is what we see!

Awakening from
an illusion is difficult
Living an illusion is depressing.

Awakening,
mind melts into spirit.

Love and Truth

Any philosophy that isn't loving, isn't true.

Enlightenment means the extinction
of the one who wants to be enlightened.

Guilt

All anger is an attempt
to make someone else
feel guilty.

Guilt can only exist in relationship to
an unforgiven past.

Guilt is a trap
which imprisons us in time.

Enlightenment

I would rather say,
"I'm not enlightened"
and be wrong about that
than to say,
"I am enlightened"
and be wrong about that.

If I condemn my brother
I place a crown of thorns upon my head,
and I nail myself to an old and rugged cross.

It is all about remembering
what we already know.

Life is neither accidental nor arbitrary.
Do not push the river.
Let destiny unfold.

Mindfulness calls for presence
where all things are joyous.

Mindlessness sees sin.
Mindfulness sees oneness.

Never give anything outside of you
power over you!

No one can hide from anything
—most of all themselves.

No sparrow falls, nor does an ameba die
without our Father's knowledge.

Not needing to exist,
we become aware of the whole of existence.

If I judge you as lower than me,
I put myself down.

Perfect vision does not see sin.
It cannot see what is not there.

It's About Time

Time is the ego's way of keeping
everything from happening at once.
We have all the time in the world because
we are not of the world.

Present in the moment, no guilty past abides,
and no fearful future can hide.

There is no difference between us except in time
and in so far as there is no time,
there are no differences.

Time is a back-flash and the older
you get the more back-flashing you
can do because you have more back
to flash at.

There is no time
in the Eternal Mind.

The past is a memory.
The future is a dream.
In the present
are we all set free.
Wherever you are—be there!
If I cannot be happy here and now.
It is for sure that I cannot be happy where I am not.

Procrastination is an avoidance of now.

Realization of the Self
is acknowledging what is not.
Remember:
What God wants you to do
is what you want to do.

St. Francis who was not interested
in owning anything loved everything and was,
therefore, incredibly rich.

Selfishness = Depression
Self-fullness = Joy

A Course in Miracles

This is a required Course.
Life is not an elective.

I am trying to learn the Course
so, I can live the Course without trying.

The Course uncovers a lie hiding inside.
The ego likes to be crucified.

Practicing the Course
means to stop blaming ourselves.
We then inevitably cease blaming others.

The moment we enter the world of words
the world begins.

The most important thing is to be sure
that the most important thing is the most
important thing

Sight gives light.
The omnipresent sees without question.
The only way out
is owning up.

Whenever I have run into a block,
I have found the detour was the right road

SUNDAYS WITH MUNDY

You cannot help but make the right decision
even when it is the wrong one. Truth always wins.

The truth undoes what never was.
There is no other Will than His which is Ours.
To get upset about another's insanity is insane.

True discipleship is remembering
what we really want.

Trust me. We all know more
than we think we do.

Truth is always defenseless.

Truth is happiness—
and hiding is despair.

Until we bring the dark to the light,
we're at the mercy of the dark.

Use the mind to go beyond the mind.

We are happy to the degree
 to which we are free.
We are free to the degree
to which we do not hide.

We do not much of the time
even attempt to control the mind.
God is hiding out in the present.

We manifest what we make judgments about,
and we will continue to manifest everything we make
judgments about until we stop judging what we manifest.

You can only get there by being here.

We walk down different paths, over different hills,
and through different valleys and, the closer we get to home
the more our roads merged into one.

What I attack in you
is the sin I see in me.

Jon's Sayings

What we see in this world is only the outer crust,
 the shell, the skin.
The ego sees a world of sin.
All the while, a loving heart beats deep within.

Whatever path you choose,
 you must work it so it can work you.

When it is cold, water freezes into ice.
When it is warm, ice turns into water.
The separated minds freeze into ego.
 An awakening mind melts back into essence.

When the world appears, the Self disappears.
When there is no guilt there is a present—clearly seen
so beautiful, free, and wholly clean.

Trying to destroy the ego makes the unimportant real.
Without the ego there would be no guilt.
Without guilt there would be no ego.

One-Mindedness Brings Loving Kindness.

Thank you for joining me on this journey.
God, says the Course, takes joy in sharing.
Covid made us go deeper by staying home.

Truth is, there is no time
and that is the end of the story.

Acknowledgments

Thanks to my darling Dolores,
for her ever-present love and devotion.
My assistant Eileen Katzmann is the best.
It was her idea to begin these epistles.
Karen Boerner edited further and brought the piece together.
Lynn Matous and David Brown proofread everything I write, and
Heather Harris added her revisions.
Thanks also to my publishers Ronnie and Ivor Whitson
for their patience and willingness.

For a free Sunday with Mundy epistle sent out on
Sunday mornings
Contact: Jon@miraclesmagazine.org.

For a sample copy of Miracles magazine contact
Eileen@miraclesmagazine.org or call our office 845-496-9089

Jon offers regular online classes on *A Course in Miracles*
Along with *Sunday with Mundy Live"*
www.miraclesmagazine.org

Made in the USA
Middletown, DE
05 May 2023

29685537R00096